Down on the Yard: A Memoir About Crime and Gangs Inside of Prison (Life in Lockdown # 4)

Published by Glenn Langohr @
http://www.audiobookprisonstories.com

Copyright 2013 by Glenn Langohr, Amazon Edition
All rights reserved. No part of this publication may be reproduced, transmitted, copied or scanned in any form or by any means, without prior written permission by the copyright holder.

This book is based on true events in the author's life. Some timelines, events, places and names have been changed to protect the innocent and the not so innocent.

Introduction

My name is Glenn Langohr. Before becoming a best selling author, I was a runaway from a broken home who fled violence from my father. I covered up emotional pain with angry chips on my shoulder that the drug war distracted. At 15 years old I started selling marijuana as a hustle and was successful for 3 years until the Criminal Justice system interrupted me and seized almost $30,000 in cash and product. At 18 years old and fighting my first case from the streets, I met a meth dealer and found a way to ignite my hustle.

I got stuck in the cycle of chasing money and power and rationalized that I had no other choice. My business partners evolved into Mexican Mobsters, Outlaw Bikers and Drug Smugglers because they were all zeroing in on the best meth cook around, my partner "King Pin Bob". To keep things ordered to my satisfaction I had to "put in work" and that consisted of drug debt collections, in home invasions and violence.

I should have learned my lesson after beating organized crime charges and the threat of a life sentence on my 3rd trip to prison. I should have outgrown those emotional issues after serving many years in prison where I was involved in riots, stabbings and solitary confinement, but I didn't.

This story finishes up my 4th prison sentence, an 11-year term. I was sent to Centinella, AKA "Sent-to-hella", on the California border of Mexico in Imperial Valley. It's a level 3 and 4 prison and as serious as they come. The prison features stabbings and riots all the time. It stays on lock down more than 9 months out of 12. The White inmates only hold 8% of the population on all four yards.

On D yard, a few months before I got there, a White inmate serving a life sentence caused a race war by stabbing a Mexican in the neck over a heroin deal. That caused another riot on the yard that made the news and everyone saw 18 White inmates lying unconscious on stretchers being rushed to ambulances. As fate would have it, I was sent there. The one good thing, my long time friend and homeboy Damon, AKA Rott, was also with me.

Rott has a bullet shaped head. He is tall and shredded with muscle. He's blasted down with prison ink and on his chest there is an Ace of Spades hovering above a three-leaf clover. He's a leader of men. We've been to war before.

On the way to D Yard we met a couple of Security Escort Prison guards named Heart and Ligazzaro. Deep, integral communication was established immediately. Heart told us about the yard politics and a current, ongoing war between the Black and Mexican inmates. A few days later he helped us get a cell move right next to the Mexican Mobsters on the yard to conduct diplomatic relations. He also told us about a couple of White inmates who were predators. One was a wife beater who had a cruelty to children charge. I stabbed him. The other one was a notorious child molester. We sliced his face.

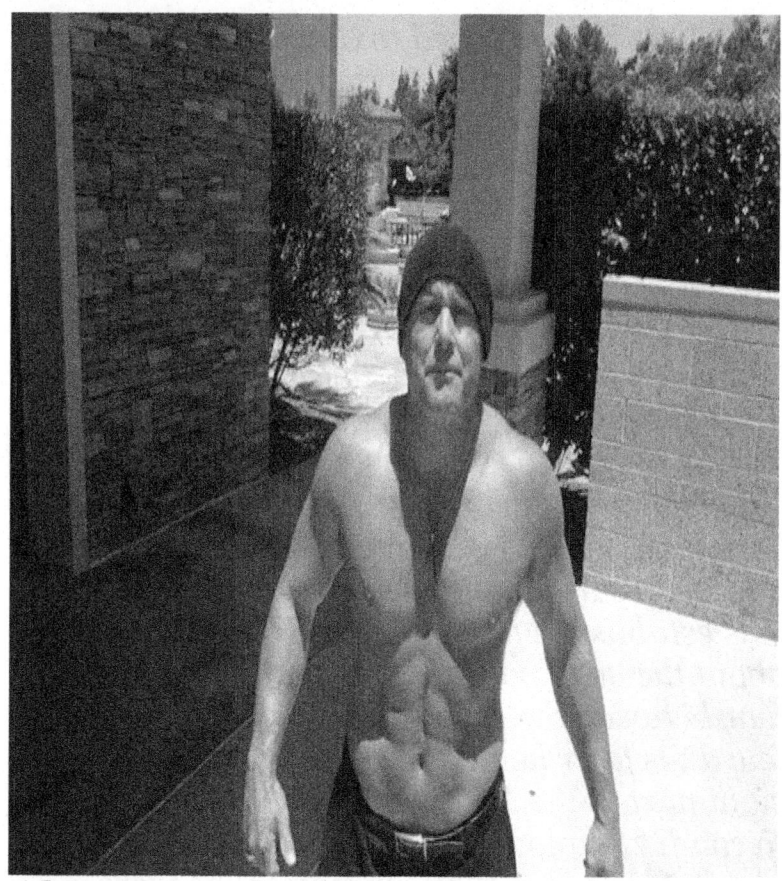

Glenn Langohr "BJ": After his release from Prison

A recap from *The Art of War: Life in Lockdown Book 3*

Down on the Yard

I pulled my line in from Boxer's cell. Attached inside a brown lunch bag were three state razors. In the message to him asking for them, I let him know what we had to do, by saying the yard was "going down" for a hot one.

It was time for vigilante justice on a notorious child molester one of the prison guards told us about.

I rolled up my mattress to expose the sheet metal bunk for Damon and I to sit on to construct our weapons.

We emptied two Bic pens and cut them down so they were four inches long with hollowed out cylinders.

I said, "Stick two razors in your pen facing the same way."

My razors were sticking out the open end a half-inch and the cap for the pen fit over it and closed, as if there wasn't something underneath.

I watched Damon finish constructing his tool and remembered something. When I pulled off the cap it would be nearly impossible to know which side the blades were facing, especially in the heat of the moment.

I said, "Make sure you know which side is the cutting end."

I used another pen to put a red dot on the outside of the cylinder facing the blade's edges.

The guard in the tower tapped on the microphone to alert the inmates to an announcement. *"Attention in the building!*

Bottom tier! Yard for the White and Asian inmates! Stand by!"

Cells started "popping" open down the tier below us. White and Asian inmates walked out of cells two at a time. The cells "popped" closer and closer to our cell until the last one opened beneath us.

Garcia looked normal standing at the podium. He was watching inmates meet and greet in the middle of the building where they marched into the vestibule tunnel.

It didn't look like anything unusual. But our cell never opened. The vestibule door shrieked and closed behind the last inmate and the building got quiet.

Damon said what I was wondering. "Mark couldn't get Heart to open us up."

I said, "It's coming."

There was a possibility that Heart wasn't working. Or, he wasn't going to give us the ability to maneuver him around, like he was with us.

Five minutes later our cell "popped" open.

With adrenaline surging through my veins the door slid on rollers right in front of me. I pulled it the rest of the way open and stepped out.

Boxer was standing at his cell door as usual. A weird thought took me captive. What if Daniel Dennings didn't come to yard for some reason?

I put my back to the wall next to Boxer's cell and whispered some of my fears. "One of the guards told us we have someone who molested a child 44 times. If he comes out this morning we're getting him."

Boxer scrunched up to the side of the cell and whisper asked, "Did you prove that claim with court paperwork?"

I said quietly through the gap of space, "Yep. There were a lot more charges with oral copulation, sodomy and other heinous sex offenses but for the purposes of sentencing he was convicted on the 1st and 15th of every month for all the major counts."

Boxer said, "Make sure you get away with it."

I tapped on his door with my knuckles in response and walked down the tier.

We exited the vestibule tunnel into the 110-degree desert heat. The sunlight was blinding.

We were wearing non descript state clothes that were blue denim with beanies covering our heads. Most of the inmates already on the yard were in grey shorts and a white tank top or no shirt.

We walked the asphalt track around the turn and stopped at the next corner by the pissers.

The guard in the gun tower 60 feet away, 30 feet in the air, was watching the yard directly in front of him. He wasn't paying attention to us in his extreme corner to his left.

From here we had the best vantage point of the yard and were almost in a blind spot from the guards.

Directly underneath the tower guard, there were exercise bars that consisted of 8 pull up bars in a row that ended in another 3 pull up bars facing the other way at a right angle. Inside further, there were dip bars that accompanied the pull up bars. In further, there were flat steel benches to do sit ups or other exercises on.

The first 4 bars in the row, the furthest from us in the corner, were the ones that the White and Mexican inmates shared. Without the Mexicans, there were only a dozen White inmates exercising.

Further into the yard, directly in the tower guard's view, about 50 yards away were the handball courts.

There was one wall 30 feet high. On one side the Asians played and on the other side the Whites played. The curb along the track had inmates standing up and watching or keeping score.

Building 3, where Daniel Dennings lived, was behind it. I scanned the rest of the yard looking for an inmate that fit Mark's description.

On the bottom tier there were 97 White inmates and 114 Asian inmates. It was impossible to find the child molester in the sea of inmates.

Standing on the curb next to me, Damon asked, "How are we going to do this?"

I said, "We're waiting for Mark to identify him. Then we're going to wait here and hope he comes to take a piss before yard recall."

The toilets were 20 feet away from us just inside the asphalt track where it turned the corner. I said, "When he walks there to take a piss or get a drink out of the fountain, we get him."

Damon nodded his head.

I explained further, "I want you to circle behind him on his way here. But you wait on me. Look into my eyes because I'm going to be facing you and the gun tower. When I look at you I'm either going to nod yes, or shake my head no based on where the tower guard is looking."

Damon nodded his head.

I continued, "From your vantage point you look behind me all the way to Building one to make sure nothing is wrong that way."

Mark Grisham came out of the Program Office almost 100 yards down the track. He walked the asphalt and stepped on the curb to survey the yard. He was getting used to us being posted up on the far corner and turned his head and saw us.

We watched him walk down the length of the asphalt track. Heat waves simmered from ink black concrete that cooked at 140 degrees.

Mark stopped in front of us and said, "He should be coming out any minute. He works as a janitor who cleans the showers and comes out after he's done for an hour and a half."

I nodded my head and felt a lump in my throat pressing in on me.

Mark continued, "I'm going to go over there and point him out as he comes out."

From 150 yards away we heard the vestibule door to Building 3 open right when Mark got close. A tall, older White inmate walked out of the tunnel by himself. Mark turned and looked our way and nodded his head.

Daniel Dennings walked the asphalt track toward Building 4 and followed the turn toward Building 5.

Mark followed him from 10 feet until he stopped walking the track and stepped into the yard to talk to a couple of inmates playing chess on the bleachers.

Damon said, "Come on Mark, don't be so obvious."

The inmates sitting on the bleachers must have been in Building 3 with Daniel Dennings.

Mark looked uncomfortable and finally started walking the asphalt track again. He passed inmates working out. Some were doing pushups on the curb. Others were doing calisthenics in groups of two. Other inmates walked the track in groups of two or three. A few inmates jogged.

Mark walked up to us and asked, "Do you know who he is?"

Damon said, "Yeah homeboy that was pretty obvious."

Daniel Dennings stood watching the game of chess for an hour. It seemed less and less likely the vigilante yard justice was going to happen.

During that period, my mind was a turbulent consumption of conscience. Thoughts waged a war of good versus evil. It had to be right to cut this child predators face for all the kids he had ruined. Images of little innocent faces flashed through my mind's eye. Then, I imagined their damaged soul's tormented in inner afflictions that the devil seized on. Childhoods in ruin, sexual relations altered, and future families destroyed, all because of Daniel Dennings. I remembered some of my own childhood that sent me into a rage that found solace in the drug war as an active participant. Even though I saw Daniel Denning's evil and the after math, I saw that I had no right to be his judge and the hand of violent justice. Who was I to decide if he had repented?

My pride was right there to torment me. I couldn't walk away from this job, not in a prison where retribution was demanded and violence was the only solution.

With 10 minutes left before yard was over for the morning, Daniel Dennings walked away from the chess game at the bleachers, and got back on the asphalt track and walked to us.

He was headed to the toilets.

Damon circled him and I looked at the guard in the tower. He was holding a block gun in his hand and staring the other way. I looked back at Damon right as he looked into my eyes. I gave a slight nod and pulled the cap off the pen to find the red dot.

Daniel Dennings was 6 feet from me and I let my adrenaline go and rushed him. He gasped first and responded by throwing his hands up in the air a split second after the blades connected just below his right ear and slashed downward to his chin, and then again.

Damon caught him in the next instant with a slice to the other side of his neck.

I turned at a sharp angle and marched in a hyper walk away from the toilets into the grass at an angle across the yard taking me to the handball court.

Every few seconds I turned my head to see how much time was left before the guards noticed.

I almost threw my pen shank of razors but held on as a thought struck me that there might be finger print evidence. To make that less likely, I pulled on the razors and felt a pile of facial skin that had built up, slide like goo with the razors as they came out of the pen cylinder. I dropped one razor and marched onward another 15 yards and dropped the other razor.

After I got half the distance to the handball courts from the scene I looked back again. I looked for Damon and didn't see him. I found Daniel Dennings staggering on the asphalt track under the tower waving his arms everywhere. The tower guard noticed and so did the inmates near the work out bars who scattered away from him.

A second later the alarm sounded. It screeched a high pitch whine that rose and fell in decibels.

The gun tower yelled into a microphone that sent his voice through speakers, "***EVERYONE GET DOWN!! DOWN ON THE GROUND***

FLAT ON YOUR STOMACHS! GET DOWN!"

I walked even faster with only a few seconds left before I would stand out as the last man standing. I got to the handball court wall and circled behind it in the only blind spot on the yard from the gun tower.

As I got down and sat Indian style for a second, I peeled off the blue denim jacket that had been buttoned to the chin. Underneath, I had on a white tank top like everyone else. I used the blue denim jacket like a blanket and got down on my stomach, in the prone position, like everyone else.

The sounds of each building's vestibule doors shrieking open were followed by guards running into the yard to look for action to quell.

Mark stood in front of the Program Office and watched the door open. A Lieutenant walked out, followed by a Sergeant, followed by Security Escort Heart who furnished the court paperwork.

Medics from the infirmary ran to a now lying down Daniel Dennings.

Down on the Yard! A True Prison Story About Life and Crime on the Inside of California's Penal System (Life in Lockdown Book 4)

Chapter 1

Where's My Cell Brother Damon?

The entrance to D Yard's gate opened and an army of additional prison guards marched at us carrying block guns and pepper spray canisters.

They circled Daniel Dennings and looked where he pointed, toward the toilets.

For the next hour every inmate stayed on the ground watching. Occasionally, a guard allowed inmates to move off the 140-degree asphalt in bunches to get back on the ground flat on the dirt and grass.

The fear was, that if you crawled or got up to avoid being burned, a guard might assume you were a combatant and hit you with a steel club or a blast of pepper spray. Then, you might stay in pain, dripping pepper spray, in handcuffs, for hours and hours waiting to go to Solitary.

The pace on the yard was slow and quiet. Almost everyone was trying to figure out what happened. This was a slashing that caused serious injury to the child rapist. My mind kept replaying how Daniel Dennings had staggered in shock with sections of his face sliced open.

The first prison guards to respond sat him on the ground and maneuvered him on his back but his hands kept hovering over his shredded face as if he wanted desperately to touch it, but was scared to.

Next, another wave of 6 medics rushed toward him. Behind that group another group of 4 came from the main hospital and entered the yard with a gurney sled.
Once on the sled, two medics rolled the injured child predator at a fast pace toward the yard gate. Another medic in white rode kneeling on the gurney sled also and it looked like she was pressing downward on his chest as if doing

CPR. The medic team ran past the program office and right by Heart and the rest of the prison guards.

Fear gripped me that if he died, this investigation would turn into a murder beef. Would the small handful of prisoners and couple of prison guards involved stay quiet? The prison guards would, they had even more to lose than us. But inmates doing dozens of years to life sentences might want to try to reduce that time by reaching out to a District Attorney...

I shook that thought away and said a prayer that he wouldn't die and like a guilty man with a conscience, I asked for forgiveness.

I studied the yard looking for Damon. After my part of the mission I had walked at an almost run from the corner of the yard to the handball court close to 75 yards away. I wanted distance from the crime to help me in any written reports. Lying on my stomach with other inmates, the 20 foot high handball wall was blocking my view of the crime scene.

But Damon shouldn't be anywhere near the crime scene. He should have had almost as much time as me to peel a good distance away.

Yet I couldn't see him.

Across from me was the rest of the handball court, then a grass field about the size of an interior Olympic track. I could see White inmates lying on their stomachs in the prone position awaiting orders from prison guards but Damon wasn't among them.

I scanned all the way to my left. The asphalt track was black ink, with heat waves rising off it. Inmates who made the mistake of getting down on it were begging guards nearby to get off it.

A prison guard who had already let a bunch of inmates move muttered, "You'd think by now you would know better."

One by one the inmates were allowed to move a few feet into the interior of the yard where the grass started. No Damon.

I looked for his bald, oblong, shaped like a bullet head around the curve of the track knowing he couldn't have reached that far but I had to eliminate nervous energy so I studied everything.

As the track curved past the last two buildings, I squinted my eyes against the sun glare and studied the White inmates to find my cell brother. If he ran, he might have been able to make it to our table where the White inmates congregated in front of building 5.

But there was no way he would have done that. That would have taken a 100-yard sprint down the track right under the tower guard.

Damon's 6 feet three inch, sinewy frame wasn't amongst the other inmates.

The guard in the tower yelled through a microphone, "**Everyone stay on the ground in the prone position. Don't move until you are told!**"

Inmates groaned from the heat. Some moved so they were lying on their sides like they were bunkering down for the duration.

I stayed flat on my stomach but arched up on my elbows to watch. The main gate to our yard opened and a dozen Inmate Gang Investigators known as IGI marched toward the Program office. They passed Security Escort Heart and got in a huddle around the Warden and Lieutenant.

A few minutes later the group of IGI guards broke into groups.

One group walked toward the corner of the yard where the slashing took place. Two guards had cameras and one of the other guards held crime scene tape.

I stomach crawled forward foot by foot to get to where I could see around the handball wall impeding my view.

At the toilets in the corner of the yard one of the IGI guards pointed to the ground. Another guard got close enough to take pictures. That guard followed a trail of blood and took more pictures.

One of the other guards wrapped crime scene tape around the area. He circled the toilets, the drinking fountains and the mister showers.

Another guard looked everywhere for a weapon.

I studied the area back and forth looking for my cell brother Damon and still couldn't find him.

One of the other groups of IGI guards was getting closer to me. They were stopping at groups of inmates on the ground and making them stand up.

The IGI guards were dressed in darker green military fatigues compared to the regular guards. They had black insignia stitched on their shoulders and chests that resembled tattoos. Most were steroid buff and looked like hyped up like criminals themselves.

One nearby ordered instructions to a patch of inmates.

"Give me your state ID."

"Where were you when the slashing happened?"

"What building are you in?"

"Strip down... Bend over and cough...Put your clothes back on and get back on the ground and wait for instructions."

He got to me.

"Stand up... Give me your ID... Where were you when he got sliced?"

"I was right here playing handball."

I stripped off my clothes and other IGI guards searched them. Then I bent over and grabbed my ass cheeks to spread them and coughed three times. It was the dirty ugly, standard procedure of prison life.

The IGI guards passed by to the other side of the handball court and put the Asian inmates through the drill. I resumed my search for Damon.

He had to have made it further than the workout bars. That was way to close to the crime scene. But he wasn't anywhere else. Unless he'd followed me, but didn't get as far and was just on the other side of the handball wall near the Asians.

I would have seen him when I repeatedly looked back.

I studied the workout bars just underneath the gun tower. It was hard to differentiate inmates who were lying flat on the dirt in between steel workout equipment.

I gave up looking for him and waited. The yard was silent except for the guards barking orders.

Finally, after an hour waiting for the IGI guards to search the entire yard and write down info, the gun tower announced, **"Attention on the yard! If you are housed in building 1 stand up and wait for an escort!"**

For the next five minutes inmates stood up and waited for guards to escort them to building 1. That thinned out the yard a little.

The same thing happened with building 2, then 3, then 4 and then our building. At the last moment I found Damon. He was in the middle of the workout bars only 30 feet from the crime scene!

There was only one other White inmate near him. Not good.

The guards started on the opposite end of the yard and collected inmates. They got to Damon and the other White inmate and the parade of inmates walked the track toward the building.

On our side of the yard the same thing happened and I stood up and entered a group of inmates. We all met up close to the building.

I got next to Damon and listened to him mutter under his breath, "I am so dumb... I'm a freaking lame."

I didn't understand and figured it must be his adrenaline. He should be excited that we made it. We got away clean so far.

In front of us 30 feet, the tan building had a black square of bulletproof tinted window above a green vestibule door. We could see a tower guard holding a block gun out the opening pointed down and to the side of us. Another guard watched us next to him.

The green vestibule door shrieked open on rollers and the 400 pounds of steel reverberated down the rollers for five long seconds.

Our building guard Garcia walked out and looked right at us. I could see him doing the math. We were the only inmates out from the top tier. All the other inmates on the yard were on the bottom tier. He had to be wondering how we got out and for what.

At around 30 years old, Garcia was a handsome Mexican with a GQ look, with short-cropped hair combed back. He turned his head and spoke a question into a microphone on his shoulder.

Above, the guard in the tower answered him. "They were called out to pick up their laundry."

We should both have bags of laundry in our hands.

Garcia nodded his head and his expression didn't change. He knew. It wasn't a puzzle, other than did we have someone else do it, or do it ourselves.

Garcia had told us that he was "only here for the paycheck." He told us we could "handle business on the yard, but not in the building." He'd essentially said we could do drugs, tattoo on each other, make and drink alcohol and pretty much run the prison, as long as we didn't make him look like he wasn't doing his job in front of higher ups.

The gun tower guard said, **"Get in the building and go directly to your cells."**

I followed other inmates into the narrow vestibule tunnel. Above, I looked up through a two-inch thick Plexiglas window the tower above could open to drop gas or fire bullets through. One of the guards walked at the same pace as us as we entered the building.

Above us he reiterated, **"Go straight to your cells and lock it up. The yard is on lockdown."**

Damon AKA Rott on the left and Glenn Langohr AKA BJ after prison

Chapter 2

Enter Building 1

We walked into the building. In front of us was the podium where the building guard usually sat facing the tower. Behind the podium was one of the three sets of bottom tier showers. Peeling both directions were cells stuffed with inmates studying us.

We climbed the stairs and turned left toward our cell. At the corner I saw a Mexican inmate named "Sparky" that Boxer, the Mexican Mobster, told us was the official for their race for the building. Like Boxer, Sparky had brown hair combed back in a place where 90% of the inmates shaved their heads. Other than being younger he had similar body language to Boxer.

I nodded my head to both he and his cell brother and leaned in to see what was wrong with Damon.

I asked, "What's up brother? What went wrong?"

Damon looked like he was stressed to the extreme. Taller than me by three inches, his big face was usually stoic, but was now full of worry lines through his eyes and forehead to his ears.

He muttered, "I forgot which way my blades were facing and cut the shit out of my finger."

That didn't make sense. I saw him pull off his end of things fine. Maybe he didn't actually do it and it just looked like it. I didn't see any actual blood because I split to fast.

Our cell door was already popped open. Boxer was standing at his door smiling. He nodded and said quietly, "Good to see you both."

I knocked on his door in response and tipped an imaginary hat his way and entered our cell.

27

After closing our cell door I said, "I saw you get him too, didn't I?"

Damon faced me and nodded his head yes and put his finger in the air like a kid showing his injury to make it real. He said, "I still got him but now I'm busted. How am I going to explain this to my wife and kids?"

The impact of the situation hit me full force. Surviving in prison without getting killed, maimed or catching extra time was part decision-making and part uncontrollable factors. This one could be construed as my fault. A 6'5 inch monster of an inmate who went by *Hitler* had already proposed I wasn't running the yard right by putting in work myself.

I got away with the last job...this one, maybe not so much.

I shook the thought to learn more. "What happened when the IGI guards asked you questions?"

Damon was still in shock and said, "I kept muttering to them what a lame I was. I blew it."

I asked, "Are you serious? You told them you were a lame?"

Damon looked me in the eyes and nodded and said, "Yep, I muttered it over and over."

I couldn't believe what I was hearing. Why was he even here? Shouldn't they have assumed his guilt and taken him to Solitary Confinement for an investigation?

Damon continued more calmly and explained. "I pulled the cap off my razors and forgot to look for which way the blades were facing and felt my finger slice open as soon as I put pressure on it. I didn't want to blow the assignment so I flipped it around and still held up my end."

I shook my head in wonder. What a soldier. What a dummy. I said what I felt. "Brother you should have aborted the mission and just let me handle it."

Now I wasn't thinking clearly and Damon said what I'd realized. "It wouldn't have mattered. I'd still have this fresh cut on my finger. I'm glad I did it or I'd really feel like a curb creature."

I still couldn't understand why he stayed so close to the crime scene. If he would have got to the other side of the yard it might not matter. "Why the hell did you stay so close to him?"

Damon said, "Because my first instinct was to hide my finger wound. I covered it in dirt on the weight pile to get it to stop bleeding."

It looked like it worked a little. The forefinger of his right hand was stained with hard dessert red colored dirt and you could barely see that it bled at all. Now I realized why my cell brother was stuck muttering frustration. It must have felt like an eternity waiting out the IGI guards sitting the closest to the slashing. His mind must have imagined things over and over.

I said, "I'm surprised you're even in the cell with me."

Damon looked more comfortable. Like he might have made it. He nodded his head and said, "They were pretty cool. They didn't even make a big deal out of it."

I asked, "Was that Danny Boy from Bakersfield who was right next to you? I saw you get up with one other White inmate?"

Damon said, "Yep. He might be just as busted as me. The IGI guards noticed his head was nicked from shaving. He even had a little blood on it."

I said, "That might help you. You could say you cut your hand shaving his head on the yard at the drinking fountains where it happened."

Damon said, "That's exactly what I said."

Chapter 3

The Italian Fox

We heard the vestibule screech open in the silent building. It rattled and clanked for five seconds and clicked into place with a final thud.

Fear gripped me that the IGI guards were going to pour into the building and look right at our cell. Maybe they had enough time to figure it out. I might be swooped up with Damon.

One of the guards in the tower was at the control booth and the other one stayed at the window overlooking the yard.

I said, "It's nothing or that guard at the window would have a block gun in his hand facing us."

Damon was standing next to me watching and nodded his head.

A few seconds later Mark Grisham walked in.

Mark is 51 years old and over 230 pounds at 6'2. He has a big baldhead; very expressive Italian face and a lot of smile and stress lines around his bright blue eyes. He's a veteran of the California prison system and can type. That got him a job working in the program office running the prison for the guards by typing all their paperwork.

That put him in a sketchy position of a cat and mouse game with the Warden, Associate Warden, Lieutenants, Sergeants and other staff. They were trying to pull info out of him about the yard and he was pulling info out of them about things like; when yard and cell searches were going down, what was happening with all manner of investigations, when the yard was coming off lockdown and lots more.

At first, we were highly troubled because Mark was a social butterfly of the highest order. He always had a steaming cup of coffee in his hand and a smile a mile wide. He also talked really loud, non-stop.

So far, he was doing well. We figured out the perfect balance of keeping that wide smile on his face with a side of seriousness to keep him on his toes.

With his help, through one of the prison guards, we were able to get a bed move from another building to the cell next to the Mexican Mobster Boxer.

We both waved our arms frantically to get Mark to come to our cell.

I muttered, "We won't have long before they make him lock it up."

Mark got up to the side of our cell and Damon asked the most vital question, "Did the child molester give a description?"

Mark said, "No, you guys got away with it clean."

Damon said, "No we didn't, look."

Mark stepped away from the side of the cell to look.

Damon had his finger in the air like he showed me.

Mark didn't notice at first and then realization dawned across his expressive face. He stepped back to the side of the cell and said, "You guys should be all good. Heart might be the one in trouble."

That was an absolutely ridiculous thought. If Heart was in trouble we were certainly doomed. We both exclaimed, "What?"

Mark continued, "He didn't expect it to go down so fast and the C-File was left open."

The first thing that the IGI detectives did when there was a battery or stabbing, was obtain the victims C-File.

At first all Heart did was say that Daniel Dennings had 44 counts of the worst kind of child molestation convictions. We told him we couldn't do it without the actual paperwork to prove it.

Mark continued, "Heart didn't get it himself, he had someone else do it."

It was getting worse. More people involved.

Mark whispered, "Heart wanted Daniel Denning's paperwork back to secure in the file before you guys whacked him."

That paperwork was mixed in with mine right now!

I said, "You've got to be kidding me. What's going to happen?"

Mark looked calm, without a stress in the world. His position was so much easier than ours, right now.

Mark said, "I think you guys are okay. Heart said it would all blow over. He said that the staff at this prison wouldn't investigate that hard. Nobody will want to look like they condone such a gross child molester."

This was way too much information to just relax over.

Damon said what I was thinking; "They have to take someone to the hole to make it look like they're doing their job. They'll come and get me in a few days.

The guard in the tower at the control booth tapped on the microphone signifying an announcement to get everyone's attention. He spoke into the microphone, "**Grisham! Lock it up!**"

We heard Mark's cell pop open on rollers 7 cells away to our left. Mark knocked on the cell door and said, "I'll be out of my cell later to type up the paperwork hopefully."

Damon stood right in front of me and said, "We have to flush Daniel Denning's paperwork."

I shook my head no. I wasn't sure if it was pride, or if it was an instinct that it might be necessary to prove something. I said, "We do have to get rid of it but how bout I send it next door?"

Damon tilted his head sideways in a new look of thought process. He decided and said, "Go for it. Just get it the hell out of here."

Damon started pacing the cell and talking out loud to process everything and for feedback.

I got on the ground facing the cell door. To my left, where our toilet was I scooped up our fishing line and unrolled it. I held a single serving milk carton container that had been folded and flattened to the width of two quarters on top of each other. Next, I stretched out about three feet of dental floss thin line. I pounded on the wall that connected our cell to Boxer's and flung the line in an arc. It circled right into his cell and smacked against his wall just inside.

I wrote a message asking for the assist. I knew he would okay it. It was a guarantee that he had a collection of written messages and evidence always at the ready to flush or stick up his ass. This would just go on top of it until we had time to figure out where to put it.

Damon said, "The IGI guard who asked me questions wrote in his report that I had a fresh cut on my finger. They'll come get me later today or in the middle of the night."

I agreed with him and said, "They will probably come get me as well. I was out on the yard when I wasn't supposed to be."

Damon said, "Maybe not. You made it to far away."

I said, "Either way. It's time to put together a care package to take to Solitary."

Usually a trip to the hole was a time to bring important things to a much more restricted place. Non-stop cell time and hardly any communication with anyone, made arriving with stuff important. You went without razors, can openers or anything else metal.

Damon said, "I'm not bringing a bunch of razors fighting a slashing beef. All I want is tobacco and lighters...and maybe something from Boxer to give to the Mexicans."

When either a White or Mexican inmate knew they were going to Solitary Confinement, it was a courtesy to help each other out and stay organized by becoming a human mule to transport messages and bring drugs or other contraband to inmates missing from the mainline action.

I wrote a message to Boxer to explain the situation and sent over Daniel Denning's court paperwork and felt relieved immediately.

I voiced what I was thinking. "We'll be alright. We won't catch cases. I know he didn't see us well enough to identify us. I looked into his eyes when I did it."

Damon paced the cell and talked while I waited for Boxer to send us a return message. He said, "I know he didn't see me either. The only extra time we can catch is for discipline by the prison."

I said, "Hopefully this just blows over and we don't even catch that."

Boxer tapped on the wall and I pulled his line in and read the message to Damon.

Greetings BJ and Rott: Glad you made it for now. You better slow your roll or you'll both be yanked to solitary and I won't have anyone to talk to. I will put something together for you to take to the hole after the work out routine. You guys ready?"

Damon said, "He's a gangster. Nothing messes up the routine for them."

I pounded on the side of the cell and yelled, "We're always ready hommie."

Boxer yelled out of his cell, *"**Spencer on the tierra! It is now time for our routina! Is everyone ready?**"* Mexican prison slang for, "Excuse me on the tier…"

All the Mexicans in the building yelled out in unison, ***"WE'RE READY!!"***

There were over 80 Mexicans in the building and their response sounded like thunder. Every building on the yard could here it.

Down the tier to our left, right next to Mark's cell, Sparky yelled out, ***"FIRST GROUP, 100 JUMPING JACKS, READY…BEGAN!"***

The sounds of bodies jumping inside of all the cells reverberated in the quiet building. In front of me, Damon was doing his jumping jacks wearing only his white boxer shorts.

Sparky yelled out, ***"SECOND GROUP, READY…BEGAN!"***

I got in front of Damon and began my set of warm-ups. At my 57th jumping jack the vestibule door opened. The usually obnoxious grinding sound was barely heard over the noise. I finished my set and traded places with Damon.

38

I kept watching to see who was coming into the building. Nobody.

In the tower above, the guards were standing at the window to the yard looking down.

Instead of anyone walking in the building, an army of 9 guards entered the gun tower one after another.

It was all the building guards for the entire yard, along with Heart and Ligazzaro. That meant they were planning on an extended lock down.

Sparky yelled out, **"FIRST GROUP, 75 PUSH UPS! READY...BEGIN!"**

Damon understood what was happening in the gun tower and said, "That's pretty obvious. They know we did it."

Damon did his pushups leaving me standing and wondering. Were they all in our building to signify they knew this is where the shot callers were?

Heart and Ligazzaro stood at the tower window watching the yard. They were probably watching the guards search for weapons using metal detectors.

In the tower, I noticed building 5's guard, Gomez, standing next to two other guards who looked like they were from Mexico. They all had the same south of the border look.

Gomez had threatened us that he could have us shot by the gun towers. A warning not to go to buildings 3 or 4 followed up that threat. Heart and Ligazzaro walked us from Gomez's building to this cell and confirmed that it was to be taken seriously.

Gomez was standing at the tower window looking right at us.

Sparky yelled out of his cell, *"**NEXT GROUP, READY...BEGIN!**"*

I did my pushups and thought about the yard. The power structure among the guards running the yard was split up into factions. Heart and Ligazzaro were in charge of escorting inmates on C and D yard like security guards. They had a good style in that while walking inmates, they shared important information and got the same in return at times. They were in the know about a lot of inmate business because of it. It gave them a feeling of power because they knew things that would happen before the rest of the prison guards. In a way, they were controlling the direction of the action at times.

Then there was Gomez and his crews of prison guards who drove from Mexico every day to work and banded up like another gang. Gomez had already shown that he liked having power and had ruthlessly instigated both the Mexican and Black inmates against each other. I was betting it was to keep the lock down going to continue to get paid time and a half for hazard pay, besides how much easier it was to run a prison locked down.

Sparky yelled out of his cell, **"SURENOS, RAZA! COMO SE SIENTE?"** *Mexican prison slang for southern mafia, Mexican race, how do you feel?*

All the Mexicans inside cells yelled with the loudest response yet. **"ONE HUNDRED PERCENT!"**

Sparky asked again to lift the crescendo of power even higher, **"HOW?"**

The response was even louder and the building thundered, **"ONE HUNDRED PERCENT!"**

Sparky yelled out, **"THAT'S RIGHT!"**

Sparky yelled out, **"WHITE RACE, HOW DO YOU FEEL?"**

Damon and I yelled, **"ONE HUNDRED PERCENT!"**

With only two of us, the response wasn't anywhere near as intimidating. But the message was out, we had just pulled up to this prison and things were changing, fast.

All the guards in the tower were looking at our cell. Some were talking to each other about it.

The workout routine went on for another 45 minutes. We did burpies, squats, leg lunges, knees to chest, chain breakers, arm rotations, kick outs, and ended with a lot more pushups.

When the routine ended, in the now quiet building, the vestibule door screeched and rattled open.

While the rest of the guards in the tower went back to their buildings to get ready for shift change, Heart and Ligazzaro walked into the building and toward our cell.

Ligazzaro stopped at Mark's cell and we listened.

Ligazzaro said, "You'll be getting popped after dinner to do the paperwork."

From the corner of our cell we watched Heart walking. He didn't even look at us. He passed us and turned on a dime at Boxer's cell.

Heart positioned himself so his back was against the wall facing the gun tower so he could whisper into the side of Boxer's cell. We couldn't hear him.

Ligazzaro walked past us also and stood facing Boxer. He didn't look at us either.

Less than a minute later we heard Boxer say, "Gracias."

The two Security Escorts walked out of the building. We listened to the vestibule rattle insane noise in the deathly quiet building until it clanged home.

Boxer immediately yelled out the side of his cell door, **"Sparky I'm sending my line!"**

Sparky yelled out immediately, **"Alright hommie!"**

Everyone knew something of great magnitude was underway. The tension in the building was so thick with anticipation; you could cut it with a prison knife.

Boxer's line flew past our cell and stopped right in front of Sparky's corner cell. Information was passed back and forth many times.

Damon said, "Boxer is telling Sparky how to deal with something."

I said, "I wonder what the hell Heart told him?"

Chapter 4

Gomez the War Monger

We found out five minutes later. Boxer sent his line into our cell asking for a cigarette. We sent one over and asked what bomb Heart dropped in his lap.

His return message told us that Gomez or his crew in the other buildings was going to unlock the Mexican and Black inmates at the same time for showers. It was going to keep the race war going. It was going to keep their two races on lockdown.

It was the perfect time to try something like that. Now that the White inmates were also on lock down, it would take more time to run showers separately. It would be more common for a mistake to be made trying to differentiate every cell.

Damon said, "Gomez is going to get stabbed for sure."

I had seen Mexican Mobsters order hits on guards like Gomez for instigating violence and continued disrespect. There was always so much pressure among the street gangs that there were always soldiers on standby for those kinds of missions. Usually when someone got in trouble that was the way to fix it.

Dinner Time

Usually dinner was brought in silver carts about the size of a portable bathroom for construction workers. The food in them wasn't much better.

It was also usually brought between 4 and 6 in the evening by all the building and yard guards in a procession that pushed about 7 or 8 carts inside to feed all 200 prisoners per building.

At 8'oclock, the vestibule finally screeched and clanked open. Instead of hearing a procession of carts squeaking and all the guards talking, it was quiet.

Damon said what I was thinking, "Bag lunches."

Two building guards walked through, each carrying a cardboard box of lunches. Another guard behind them had one in his hand and was pushing another one on the ground with his foot.

I said, "They didn't have anyone to work in the chow hall to make our food."

While the initial investigation took place on the slashing, all the inmates were locked down. Soon, it would be deemed that there wasn't any racial tension and it was a White on White issue.

The Asian inmates would be the only inmates allowed to go to yard and run the prison functions like the kitchen.

After the lunches were passed to every cell, Mark Grisham's cell door popped open.

The gun tower at the podium tapped on the microphone and announced, **"Grisham, they need you in the program office."**

Chapter 5

No Sleep for the Restless

Damon did what I usually did. He paced the cell non-stop, back and forth, like an animal marking space.

I tried to read the Bible and couldn't concentrate. So I resorted to humor to loosen up.

I leaned over and watched my cell brother. I imagined our cell and the entire building like a fish tank. It had to look and feel like that to the guards in the gun tower.

I said, "If you were a fish swimming back and forth from one end of the tank to the other, I'd say you look like an Arowana."

Damon stopped for a second and studied me. His face was back to his normal stoic, frozen irritated. He was processing all the information and coming to terms with it. A tiny smile fractured minimally across his face and he asked, "What's an Arowana?"

I said, "It's a freshwater bony fish that is so territorial, it swims the length of the tank, back and forth, continuously, just like you're doing now."

Damon's smile increased and he started pacing again. He said, "Tell me more about this Arowana."

I said, "Its one of the oldest fish on record and can be traced back over 200 million years to Africa and South America."

Damon couldn't hold it in. I saw and heard a lot of the pressure releasing from him in the form of laughter. He said, "Tell me more."

He took a glance at me as he paced. I had a stone cold serious expression while I continued, "They're very protective of their young and are known to hold hundreds of eggs in their mouths. The young start off by taking several tentative trips outside the parents mouth to investigate the surroundings before leaving permanently."

Damon laughed even harder and said, "You're making this up homeboy!"

In all seriousness, I shook my head and said, "No its true. I saw it on the Discovery channel."

Damon shook his head and kept pacing. He asked, "What else?"

I let him pace back and forth a few times and continued, "Their feeding patterns are quite unusual. In the wild they are known to eat insects and birds."

Damon didn't believe me. He kept pacing and said, "Yeah right homeboy, I'm not buying this crap."

He stole a glance at me and I nodded my head it was so.

I kept a very serious face and continued, "It's true. Like you, the Arowana are excellent jumpers and leap out of the water and pick their food off branches along the Amazon River."

Damon shook his head, no way.

I continued, "They also have an AKA like you. But instead of Rott they go by "Water Monkeys.""

Damon stopped pacing. It looked like he was deciding that I wasn't messing with him.

He tried another tactic to see if my expression would change and said, "I believe you. Tell me more."

Instead of pacing, he was studying me intently. He wanted to see how far I could take it.

Since I was telling the truth, it was easy. I said, "In captivity, like us, adults show a lot of dominance and aggression. They are only compatible with other aggressive fish as long as they can't fit in their mouth."

Damon shook his head in shock and said, "You got all that from the Discovery Channel?"

I said, "Not all of it, my brother had one in his tank for a while and I researched it on Wikipedia."

He said, "Your freaking serious aren't you."

I said, "No B.S. I'm serious as a heart attack."

Damon started pacing again and muttered to himself, "I remind him of an Arowana."

Three hours of nervous pacing later, the vestibule door shrieked open.

We watched a guard in the tower walk with a block gun in his hand at the same pace of whoever was walking through the tunnel.

Mark Grisham walked into the building and looked right at our cell. He was walking fast. He wasn't smiling.

The guard in the tower at the podium tapped on the microphone and said quietly, "Lock it up Grisham."

His cell popped open.

At the stairs Mark turned around, looked up and said, "Can you give me a shower?"

The guard said, "Not tonight."

Mark shook his head and said, "Can you give me one minute?"

The guard said, "You have 30 seconds."

Mark got to our cell and said, "I typed all the reports. He didn't say anything or give any description. He wouldn't even say if it was a White inmate."

Damon asked, "Do you think we're going to the hole tonight?"

Mark said, "I don't know. Heart thinks you might before long."

The guard in the tower said, "Lock it up Grisham!"

Chapter 6

So Far, No Penalty Flags

I woke up to the sounds of shift change at 4 am. It started with the vestibule clanging and reverberating down the rollers and ended in a bang. Next were the sounds of keys dangling and jangling off the sides of the new building guards as they walked in. Then the sound of one of the guards running up the stairs in the otherwise quiet, sleeping building.

The guards in the gun tower were half asleep. That meant breakfast was going to be bag lunches and not for a while.

Four hours later the inmates in the building started normal activity.

One Black inmate yelled from downstairs and across the way, "Yo T-Bone! This is Cadallac cuz! Send me one of doz books you tole me about and some afro sheen!"

T-Bone was to the right of us a couple of cells and he yelled back, "Which one cuz?"

That conversation got other conversations started and for the next hour everyone started their day in lock down.

An hour later inmates started yelling at the guards.

A Black inmate yelled, "Tower! Where's our food?"

Another Black inmate yelled, "When we gonna get showers?"

No response.

An hour later the vestibule clamored and screeched open. Garcia and another guard walked through the tunnel with boxes of bag lunches.

Garcia came up stairs with a box and the other guard went to the corner cell on the bottom tier.

He got to our cell and it popped open. He handed us four bag lunches and said, "Breakfast and lunch."

I asked, "When are they going to decide this lock down?"

Garcia said, "You guys will be locked down this week for sure. They're going to hold another meeting about it next week. The Asians are going back to work today and getting off lock down tomorrow."

Chapter 7

Meditative Mode

We got used to the lockdown fast. It was time on a shelf, in slow motion, meditation. To give Damon some sort of space in the cell, I woke up at 4 am and took a mid day nap.

Damon woke up at 10 am and went to sleep later than me by six hours.

The time we spent in the cell awake together was for taking turns standing at the cell door studying everything, working out, playing chess, pacing the cell and reading.

The only time we came out of our cells was for showers.

The Black inmates were giants compared to the Mexican inmates. Another thing the Black inmates had going was that most of them were veterans of the California prison system. They all looked like they had 10-20 years of high level, maximum-security experience.

The Mexicans had a collection of experience mixed with younger, less seasoned inmates. They were broken up into southern California Mexicans, most of who were straight gang bangers who claimed streets, and Mexicans from Mexico, who were mostly drug smugglers. Boxer was in charge of all of them.

We watched the bottom tier shower. Down below, two Black Crip gang members swaggered down the tier at a snail's pace. Both were yelling to other Black inmates inside cells.

Damon said, "The Black inmates here seem pretty unified."

It was hard to tell the difference between the Black Crips and Bloods until you looked closely. The difference was spelled out on bodies in tattoo ink but it was hard to read on their black skin. The other indicators were body language attributes, like the Crip walk-swagger, the sagging pants with many pairs of sagging boxers even lower, and the lingo used like,

"Crizzip, Cuz and the extra zip sounds on everything.

The Bloods tended to be a little older and at times much more dignified.

The Crips outnumbered the Bloods in a big way and they often fought against each other, just like the southern Mexican street gangs fought over control. In both cases, they united against other races when it was time for war.

Underneath, the two Crip gang members stopped at different cells right next to each other.

They stayed there for over five minutes instead of showering.

The guard in the tower tapped on his microphone and said, ***"You have five more minutes for the shower whether you get in there or not!"***

The two Black inmates didn't even look. They kept talking for a couple more minutes. Then they swagger stepped to the middle downstairs showers.

We watched the Black inmates finish getting showers for the next couple of hours.

Damon asked, "I wonder if we're going to hear the alarm going off today?"

I studied Garcia sitting at the podium and answered, "Probably soon. I wonder if Gomez or one of his friends in the tower are going to pop out a bunch of cells of Mexicans with only one or two Blacks out."

Damon grunted and said, "Probably."

We were both wrong.

Chapter 8

A Longer Lockdown Means More Easy Money

Building 3 where the child molester Daniel Dennings used to live was a less political building than all the rest of the buildings. It was the only building where inmates who wanted to take medications for mental issues were housed.

Tower guard Torrez sat at the podium getting ready to unlock cells for showers. He tapped on the microphone and said, **"Attention in the building! Shower time for the Black, Mexican and White inmates! When your cell is popped go directly to the showers. You only have 5 minutes so we can get through everybody!"**

Tower guard Bonitez stood at the tower window holding a block gun with half of it out a portal opening pointed at the ground.

Tower guard Torrez tapped on buttons and six cells popped open.

Below, the Mexicans knew what time it was. The first problem, only one cell had Mexicans in it and the other five cells had Black inmates.

Another problem, the one Mexican cell that popped open held two non gang banging, older and weakened, Mexicans from Mexico.

All the other Mexicans in cells were standing at the door with so much intensity that it tipped off an aware Black Crip gang member who came out of his cell first.

He got spooked and he yelled a warning, "Heads up Crizzips! Somptings about to crack a lack!"

That caused even more anticipation and the tension shot up so high it did pop.

The 10 Black inmates turned as one group a few feet in front of the cells. The first Crip to yell a warning was the closest to the Mexicans standing there looking overwhelmed. He threw his hands in the air and yelled, "Want some? Get some!"

That was enough to push the two Mexicans over the edge and they rushed in.

Each Mexican was under 160 pounds and over 50 years old, but they had heart.

The Black inmates opened up and swarmed. The first Black Crip swung wild haymakers and connected with the first Mexican.

The entire building had inmates yelling from their cells and it was mayhem.

Inmates slammed their metal cell door with plastic cups. Some kicked cell doors. It sounded like a thousand pieces of hail slamming the roof of a car.

The rest of the Black inmates pounced on the two Mexicans. Both Mexicans took punches from multiple angles and went to the ground like a sack of potatoes.

The sounds of a one sided thumping filled the building.

Some of the Black inmates got down low and fired punches unobstructed against both of their adversaries heads. The other Black inmates pummeled them with soccer style kicks to all parts of the now folded up Mexican bodies.

The action continued in the one sided smashing for thirty more seconds and one of the Mexicans went limp into unconsciousness.

The other one covered tighter in the fetal position with his arms wrapped around his face and head against the unending assault.

Nobody in the building paid any attention to the drowned out alarm that screeched decibels in a high-pitched whine over and over. Nobody even heard the vestibule screeching open.

Everyone saw the army of prison guards pour into the building.

The guard at the gun tower screamed with more and more urgency into the microphone, ***"GET DOWN! GET DOWN! FACE DOWN ON THE GROUND!"***

The other guard in the tower fired his block gun, **"BOOM!"**

He set that gun down and picked up another one and fired, **"BOOM!"**

The melee was 30 feet away and the block gun bullets opened up to far to be effective. The pieces of blocks bounced off the back of one of the fighting Black inmates.

The army of prison guards rushed the inmates and released a stream of pepper spray out of canisters the size of fire extinguishers. Black inmates were dripping with orange spray and yelling obscenities. One by one they started getting on the ground.

The first Black Crip to the fray wasn't done. By himself, he landed a few more kicks to the unconscious Mexican, moving his lifeless body.

The closest guard on the floor with a block gun fired from 10 feet away. **"BOOM!"**

Up close, the block projectile did damage.

It hit the Black combatant in the back and his body surged forward and onto the ground. He gasped with the wind knocked out of him and reacted by jerking his body.

A guard closing in took that as an opportunity to hose pepper spray on him.

The only noise left of the skirmish was coming from prison guards.

*"**STAY ON THE GROUND! DON'T MOVE AN INCH!**"*

Chapter 9

Three Days Later

Mark Grisham Explains

Mark finished telling the story as he heard it from Security Escort Heart.

Damon said, "Gomez is a punk ass bully."

Mark said, "Heart wants his ass!"

Hearing Mark say that irritated me. Mark had also told us that Heart was frustrated with us for the way we handled the business on the Child Molester.

Mark should have been pissed off at Heart, for forcing us to stab people by providing information about a sex offender and another predator. He should have been pissed off at Heart for being sloppy by leaving the C-file open. This might cost us extra prison sentences and a lifetime in Solitary confinement.

Damon said, "Screw Heart. He doesn't have to do any of the work, but we pay the price."

Mark nodded his head and changed his expression. He said, "You guys handled it faster and more serious than he expected. He got caught slippin."

I asked, "What's up with our lockdown?"

Mark said, "We'd be off if there wasn't two stabbings in a row. Now they have to run investigations."

That meant that they had to cover it up with paperwork in case Sacramento looked into it.

Mark said, "They're starting today in Gomez's building. They'll be interviewing in those offices down there when they get to our building."

Mark pointed toward the vestibule, where an office was underneath the gun tower.

Chapter 10

The Noose is Squeezing My Neck

Warden Pickler stared across his desk at Lieutenant Deadwood and CC2 Jackson. He said, "I don't want to push the issue either but since the victim's C-File was left wide open and the IGI wrote that in their reports we have to do this."

The machismo in the room was started. Lieutenant Deadwood said, "I'm glad that the child molester got his face carved on, I would kill him if he violated my kids. I sure don't want to see any inmates catch extra time for doing society a service."

Warden Pickler nodded his head and said, "I have kids also and understand, but like I said, we have to do our job."

CC2 Jackson had seen a lot. He was a veteran of the California Prison Industrial Complex. He started at Folsom, went to Soledad, then Pelican Bay when it opened and then came to Calipatria and now Centinella. A Black man originally from the streets of Chicago, everyone liked him, prison staff and inmates alike, for his authenticity. He was a human being who cared.

Jackson said, "Unless someone talks, this is all for show anyway. Lets get started."

The procession walked out of the program office and passed Mark Grisham in a cubicle typing reports.

Mark heard everything and got up to talk to Security Escort Heart in the next room.

Heart was playing cards with Ligazzaro when Mark knocked on the door. He yelled, "Come in!"

Mark opened the door and stepped inside. He said, "Sorry to bother you guys but I just heard the Warden leave with the Lieutenant and Jackson. They're starting the Q and A in five block."

Heart kept his cards to his chest and said hesitantly, "And?"

Mark had been feeling BJ and Damon's pressure. He felt a little responsible for the direction things might go and wanted to do something. He asked, "What's the chances my homeboys are going to the hole?"

Heart said, "High. Someone has to go. It might be Damon and Danny who were the closest to the scene because both had fresh blood on them."

Ligazzaro nodded his head and said, "BJ might go also."

Heart nodded and said, "It might be all three but I'm betting none of them catch any extra time at all."

Ligazzaro said, "The DA won't pick it up and we won't find them guilty of anything to keep them in Solitary unless an inmate tells on them and forces us to."

Mark was frustrated. He felt used. For the first time he realized BJ and Damon were right. They were just being used as pawns and were the ones who had to pay the real price. He said, "If they go to the hole can I at least send them with a couple of lighters."

Heart looked at Ligazzaro and shook his head and said, "That would be illegal. We can't take part in that."

He reached into his pocket and took out a lighter and threw it in the garbage can next to him.

Ligazzaro shook his head also and said, "That would be considered contraband and get them an extra month in Solitary."

He also pulled a lighter out of his pants pocket and dropped it in the trashcan.

Mark smiled at the small victory. He stared at the trashcan waiting for a green light.

Nobody said anything for a minute and Mark asked, "Did you want me to take this trash out for you?"

Heart said, "Sure."

Chapter 11

What You Talkin About?

Warden Pickler, Lieutenant Deadwood and CC2 Jackson stood at the vestibule to Building 5.

Above, the tower guard looking down at them said over his shoulder, "They're here. Let em in."

The guard at the control booth opened the vestibule door and spoke to Gomez through his radio.

"The Warden is here for the investigation. Which tier do you want out first?"

Gomez got up from his podium and walked the floor to the vestibule and said, "Top tier."

The guard at the control booth tapped on the microphone to signify the announcement. **"Attention in the building! This is for the White and Asian inmates. When your cell is popped open you will be handcuffed and escorted to answer a few questions!"**

Someone in a cell yelled, ***"Or not!"***

Gomez agreed with the inmate and said, ***"No informants at this prison. This will be quick."***

Gomez met the investigative team as they entered the building. He shook each of their hands and led the way to the office a few feet to the left.

He opened the door and they all entered.

Warden Pickler took a seat at the head of the table with Lieutenant Deadwood taking the seat to his right, followed by CC2 Jackson sitting across from the Warden.

Gomez walked up the stairs to the only White cell on that side.

He said, "Inmates Smith and Wesley turn around. When the cell pops open put your hands behind your backs so I can cuff you."

Gomez walked behind the inmates down the stairs and said, "You guys won't get off lockdown any faster if you tell on who did it."

Inmate Smith, known as Traveler, said, "Did what? What are you talking about?"

Gomez laughed and said, "Tell that to the Warden and don't be in there more then a minute or people will wonder if you're talking."

65

Traveler nodded at the Warden and glanced at the Lieutenant and CC2 Jackson.

The Warden said, "Sit down you two."

Both inmates sat down.

The Warden said, "On May 5th there was a slashing on the yard. Do either of you know anything about it?"

Both inmates, in unison, said, "Nope."

The Warden asked, "Would you tell me if you did?"

Both inmates again responded together, "Nope."

The Warden laughed and the Lieutenant said, "Nobody at this prison is a rat."

CC2 Jackson said, "Especially against someone who put in work on the child molester."

Traveler needed CC2 Jackson's help. He was involved in a riot with the Mexican inmates on A yard six months ago.

CC2 Jackson was in charge of all the counselors assigned to inmates to handle all manner of administrative work. Usually, the counselors didn't do their jobs, and a seasoned inmate knew to go over his head.

Traveler said, "Mr. Jackson my counselor isn't doing his job to restore my time for that riot I was in on A Yard. I have 180 days without a write up and want that time back before it's to late."

Jackson nodded his head and remembered. He said, "Oh yeah I remember. You and inmate Rocky were back to back swinging hay makers to keep about 20 Mexicans off you."

The Lieutenant chimed in, "They were the two biggest White boys on the yard. The rest of the White boys weren't so lucky."

The Warden nodded his head at the memory and said, "Lot of serious injuries in that one."

CC2 Jackson said, "Send me the info and I'll get it to a hearing."

Gomez grabbed Traveler by the handcuffs behind him and steered him out of the office.

Chapter 12

Change In the Air

Mark walked from the program office across the yard to Building 1. He tapped his back pocket and felt both lighters and decided to camouflage them.

He pulled out a brown lunch bag out of his front pocket and placed the lighters inside and folded it tight.

Standing in front of the vestibule he got the gun tower's attention.

Above, the tower guard alerted the other guard who spoke to Garcia on the floor.

Garcia said, "We have the Warden on his way. Tell Grisham he can't talk to any inmates at cell doors. He has to lock it up immediately."

The tower guard looked down at Grisham and said, "You have to lock it up immediately."

The vestibule grinded and shrieked open and Mark walked into the tunnel.

He walked into the building right to the podium. He asked Garcia, "Can I have one minute at my homeboy's cell. They're probably going to Solitary."

Garcia shook his head no and said, "I can't let you. The Warden is walking."

Mark said, "He's just getting out of Building 5. He's a couple hours away from this building."

Garcia shook his head no again and said, "You better know sign language. You have two minutes left before you have to be in your cell. Better say good-bye with your fingers now.

Garcia and Mark turned to look up at BJ and Damon in cell 211. Both were watching.

Chapter 13

Insert The Luggage!

The vestibule shrieked open and got our attention. We both went to the cell door to watch.

The gun tower was more vigilant. He said something to Garcia right as Mark walked from the tunnel into the building.

Mark didn't look up at our cell like normal.

Damon voiced what I was thinking, "Somethins up."

Mark stayed at the podium for longer than usual with a serious expression on his face. After another minute, he turned our way and walked a few hesitant steps toward us.

He looked uncomfortable, like he didn't know what to do. Then without saying anything he lifted his hand and started finger-signing letters.

We read them out loud.

Y-O-U
B-O-T-H

M-I-G-H-T
G-O-
T-O
S-O-L-I-T-A-R-Y
R-I-G-H-T
N-O-W.

I felt anxiety rush into my stomach and with a dry throat said, "Get your luggage ready."

Mark turned towards Garcia and asked, "Can I throw this up to my homeboys?"

Garcia asked, "What is it? Never mind, I don't want to know."

Mark walked closer to our cell and threw a brown bag over the railing. It landed a few feet away from us.

I got on the ground and unraveled enough of our fishing line to throw it out and circle it and pull it in.

Damon was rifling through his prison mattress. He had a hole in it and his hand was searching a few feet into the interior for his care package.

Boxer had sent a message and a lighter to transport to another Mexican Mobster in Solitary. On top of that and in the same plastic wrapped bundle were about 40 cigarettes compressed into a tightly wrapped plastic lump. The entire package was about the size of two fingers.

I pulled out the lighters and turned to Damon and said, "Do you have room in your ass for more?"

Damon's face puckered up like he just ate a sour lemon. He said, "Why don't you take that one for us?"

I nodded my head okay but realized something. "What if we're on the opposite ends of Solitary from each other? You might not get your lighter for a long time if at all."

Solitary Confinement had cells that were set up in wings that ran away from each other. It was almost impossible to transfer messages and contraband. There were ways, but it took a long time to coordinate.

Damon said, "I can fit one more lighter."

Mark walked up the stairs and I looked back at him and finger signed, "T-H-A-N-K-S."

His face was the saddest yet. He looked like a hound dog who missed going for a walk. I yelled out, "It's alright homeboy. Nothin you could do about it."

Damon said, "Lets shoot our line to see what's happenin and when we're goin."

I yelled out, "We're shooting our line!"

A few minutes later we got a message of explanation from Mark.

Chapter 14

Here Come The Handcuffs Again

We heard the vestibule screech, rattle and shriek open for five long seconds. I realized, I might actually miss that sound in Solitary.

The sounds were going to change to giant keys inserting into heavy doors and closing like tombs.

Heart and Ligazzaro walked into the building and looked at our cell for a second on his way to the podium to talk to Garcia.

Damon noticed before I did and said, "He has his handcuffs out.

Boxer slammed on our cell wall and said, "**See you guys around the corner! Mucho gusto!**"

Next to Mark's cell, Sparky yelled out, "**You guys just got here!**"

A few other inmates we knew yelled sentiments our way while Heart and Ligazzaro walked to our cell.

Heart was all business. He said, "BJ I need you to strip down... Lift each foot and wiggle your toes... Bend over and cough three times... Put your clothes back on..."

Heart did the same thing with Damon and we were handcuffed and told to walk backward out of the cell. Heart and Ligazzaro held our elbows and guided us down the stairs and out the building. I was irritated with Heart but held a muzzle on my mouth. Who knew what kind of influence he had on additional charges being added.

Entering the yard the sunlight blinded me after not seeing it for a while. The 115-degree desert heat hit me in the face next.

I walked slowly, like a man who knew my next destination only held more extreme captivity, without sunlight.

Heart broke the silence and said, "You guys shouldn't have done that mission. You should have had someone else do it."

We decided in the cell not to say a word, lest it be used against us.

My thoughts were turbulent. Heart shouldn't have told us. He crossed the line and became a participant.

He also shouldn't play gangster business as a Monday morning quarter back. He didn't understand all the factors. From his position he assumed being a leader on the yard wasn't fraught with risks and challenges, 24-7-365.

Behind me, holding Damon's elbow, Ligazzaro said, "You guys aren't going to catch any time. This is all for show. The Warden said you aren't going to be in Solitary long."

Heart said, "In fact, you both might not go. So far it's just Damon and Danny Boy."

I asked, "Huh? What's goin on?"

Heart said, "It's up to the Warden after he finishes the interrogation. He's headed to your building next. I'm holding you in the office until then."

Ligazzaro said, "You aren't going unless someone tells on you. Damon and Danny Boy will stay in Solitary for 3-6 months."

I felt a little relief I wasn't going to Solitary, but even more apprehension that Damon wouldn't be with me to help. I asked, "Why am I in handcuffs if I'm not going?"

Heart said, "The Warden is going to interrogate you both and make a final decision."

Chapter 15

The Interrogation

It wasn't a puzzle, or even a Rubik's cube. They knew we did it. Heart probably shared the information.

The interrogation started in the Warden's office. We heard the gathering arrive into the program office. They were talking out loud for our hearing.

Someone said extra loud, "Nobody said a word about the slashing."

Another voice, "The child molester got justice."

Another voice, "I would have been disgusted with this prison if an inmate would have informed on whoever did it."

We heard a knocking on the door and Heart said, "We're in here."

A voice outside said, "Give us a minute to sit down in my office and escort them in."

The Warden was at the head of the table. At around 60 years old and White, he looked like a product of the California/Mexico border. We'd heard that his parents were involved in farming, and he elected to take a job working for the fastest growing union in California, the prison boom. He had a baldhead with big green eyes covered by prescription glasses and a good old boy, happy go lucky face.

Next to him was the Lieutenant. Another White man of around 50 years old, he was dressed in uniform and had all the insignia stitched on his arms to prove it.

Sitting across from the Warden was a Black man with a baldhead and an expressive face.

Everyone nodded at us standing in the doorway with our Security Escorts holding our elbows behind us like we were being propped up on a stage.

The Warden introduced himself, as did the others and then said, "Have a seat."

The Warden rattled off information about the incident regarding the time, date, nature of the offense, the name of the victim and the current stage of the investigation. Then he said, "Off the record, I'm glad the scum bag got regulated and don't want to see anyone pay the price for it. I know how it works in here."

It was choreographed.

The Lieutenant proved it by following up with what had to be rehearsed. "We have to take a couple people to Solitary for this because it looks bad if we don't. We know it was an inside job. There was evidence left out that force our hand. I can promise you that you won't catch extra time if you keep your mouths shut."

The Warden broke in and said, "BJ I'm leaving you on this yard after I interview you. Damon I expect you to stay in Solitary for around three months while the investigation grounds out to nothing. I put in a request for you to be in the same cell as Danny."

Damon nodded his head and swallowed and asked, "Where's Danny?"

The Warden said, "He's already in Solitary. We interviewed him this morning and asked him if he was in a gang, if he had an AKA and other questions and he took the 5th."

We were led out of the Warden's office and into another room. Damon and I were sat down while everyone else remained standing.

The Warden said, "We're starting with you BJ… Are you in a gang?"

"No."

The Warden, "What neighborhood do you run with on the streets?"

"The YMCA."

The Warden, "Is that a joke?"

"Yes."

The Warden, "Do you have an AKA?"

"Nope."

The same thing happened with Damon. The Lieutenant watched and the Black Administrative Officer took notes.

The sad, inevitable part came when I had to leave Damon. Handcuffed, I couldn't hug him. It was more of a silent, shoulder bump.

With my lips clamped down, I said, "Love you homeboy. Maybe you can come back to this yard after the investigation."

It was a hopeful thought. One I held on to.

Chapter 16

Two Is Better Than One

The first thing I did back in the cell was sit on the toilet and poop out my plastic wrap lighter. It matched my mood and I cleaned it in the sink empty of emotions.

I paced the cell and self manufactured a better mood. Walking in solitude always helped me think.

I told myself that I was used to this. I'd seen over 100 different cells all over California in almost a dozen different state prisons and three different county jails.

It could be worse. We could have really got caught. We were okay. It was a learning experience. Next time, I'm telling Heart or another Officer of the Law, no thanks, I don't want to know about any sex offenders or anything else. You are a cop, and I'll be an inmate trying to survive and find redemption.

I felt my spirit strengthen and talked to God for another 20 minutes of pacing. I made all my usual promises and thank You's and felt even better.

My workout routine came next. I did 10 sets of handstand pushups, 500 pushups and 20 minutes of jumping jacks, knees to chest and arm rotations.

Sweating out my stress, I filled the stainless steel sink with water and got naked for a cell shower.

Sitting on the toilet facing the sink, I scooped a cup of water all over my body until the sink was empty.

After a complete rinse, I used the floor towel to sop up all the water and clean the cell.

A few minutes later Mark's cell popped open.

I stood at the side of my cell studying him. He looked as depleted of emotions as I felt.

Neither one of us said anything for almost a minute. Then I said in a dejected voice, "I miss him already."

Mark nodded his head. He said, At least we know this is all for show."

That sentiment didn't help my mood. I felt cheated. I said, "If Heart wouldn't have left the C File out my cell brother would still be here."

Mark nodded his head and said, "Yep. He knows he screwed it up."

Mark had enough influence from being in the program office with the prison staff everyday to at least work on something for me. I said, "You're going to help me get Damon back in this cell with me."

Mark's face changed from a frown to confused. He asked incredulously, "How?"

I said, "We're going to have to wait until he sits out the investigation in Solitary but then we're getting him back here."

Mark shook his head no and said, "They never let someone come back to the same yard."

He was wrong. It all came down to the victim. In this case, since it was a stabbing, the victim would leave the entire prison. I told Mark.

He said, "You're right."

I continued the education and said, "It's like this, they all know we did it and probably know Heart had it done. You just hit Heart up on how to get it done."

The guard in the tower tapped on the microphone and announced, "**Grisham get to the program office.**"

Chapter 17

What Am I Going To Do Now?

A couple hours later the vestibule shrieked and rattled open. Mark came striding into the building and looked at me. He was smiling.

He scrunched up to the side of the cell door and said, "Heart said it's possible. He told me to wait for a while and he would get CC2 Jackson to okay it. He's the lead counselor for the entire yard."

So I was three to six months away from possibly getting my cell brother back. My mind analyzed so many possibilities.

It was going to be harder for me to run the yard for the White inmates without him. Damon had a lot of influence with the Skin Heads. I had a lot of influence with the Mexicans. It had been a perfect fit.

Mark said, "We're getting off lockdown tomorrow now that the investigation is over."

I nodded my head and felt a little anxiety without my right hand man.

Mark asked, "Do you want the Barber job? You can get to both yards that way."

It was my first chance to face the fear full blast. If I took the barber job I would always be able to get out of my cell and the building, as long as the yard wasn't locked down. I voiced the only problem, "I don't know how to cut hair."

Mark said, "Not a problem. You only have to use the clippers to shave heads. Plus everyone knows you have the yard and they will respect that you need to be able to get around."

With the barber job I would be able to get in every building. It would show everyone I was more than willing. I said, "I'll do it. Get me the job."

I paced the cell for the rest of the day thinking. Each race had a Barber that picked up a plastic box of clippers from the lead yard guard every morning. From there, the Barber was able to walk that box to any of the five buildings or the gym to get inside. The Barber not only cut hair, he could transport information rapidly, broker peace, or war and also transport weapons or drugs. It was a high-pressure job.

Chapter 18

Yard Is Open For the White Inmates

The next morning started with an announcement from the tower guard. ***"Attention in the building! Yard release for the White and Asian inmates! Top tier get ready for release."***

I walked through the vestibule with as much confidence as possible. In prison, perception is reality. If I put off the scent of confusion, it would magnify and inmates would pick up on it.

The yard was empty. I walked the asphalt track that circled the baseball-sized field of a yard. To my right the track circled the edge of the yard where razor wire topped cement walls sealed out the surrounding desert.

The next building in front of me was the chow hall. White and Asian inmates stood watching me behind doors. I stopped at the corner of the track and looked to where the slashing happened.

The toilets, mister showers and drinking fountains were just inside the track, 20 feet away. My mind flashed images of how the child predator walked toward the toilets just before we got him. I shook the images away and knew they would never completely leave.

Another memory invaded while I looked past the toilets into the yard grass. About 20 feet away was a sprinkler where we buried a couple of shanks. They made it through the yard search and all the metal detectors because they blended in with the noise the metal sprinkler made.

The tower for the entire yard was directly over the gym and sat 30 feet in the air with the best view of the yard. His vision was straight ahead to Building 3. It was the Mexican, ex military sharp shooter. To look at me he had to turn his head to his extreme left. I was stationed in his blind spot. I stayed still to detect the pulse of the yard.

Inmates marched out of Buildings 2 and 3. The White inmates were larger than the Asian inmates. They also had a completely different walk and body language.

The White inmates were instructed to start at the only White table on the yard. It was the only way to hold space to stay organized. Once the Black and Mexican inmates were off lockdown, if we didn't hold our table, Mexicans would take it over and we wouldn't have anywhere to congregate and stay on top of things as a group.

Buildings 4 and 5 opened next. Inmates came pouring out. The guard in the tower studied them to detect body language and the tension level.

Satisfied that the inmates were just going to yard, to work out, play handball or cards, he turned his head to the extreme left and was surprised to see me by myself, staring at him.

I responded by stepping off the curb and got into a pushup position and went into a set.

50 pushups later I got up and did some shoulder rotations. I glanced up at the guard; he was busy studying the yard elsewhere again.

I went down for another set and heard someone banging on the door to the chow hall behind me.

While doing pushups I was able to look behind me, under my body, but couldn't make out who was at the door.

After the set I got up and turned around. It was Jeremy.

So far Jeremy had been a bright spot in an otherwise hellacious environment. At 23 years old, he adapted to prison life fast. *His father was the President of the Mongol's Biker gang, but that didn't give him status in California prisons where bigger street gangs and the mafia ruled.* His respect was earned because he hustled by smuggling some of the morning juice from breakfast that was shared with inmates who converted it into wine. He also smuggled in money from his grandmother who folded a hundred dollar bill as tight as possible and wrapped a few balloons around it so he could swallow it during each visit. He used that money to purchase a can of Buglar tobacco from a prison guard through another inmate from Bakersfield known as Yard Dog Mike.

Jeremy smiled at me and used his fingers to sign through the window.

U-
G-O-T-
A-W-A-Y-
D-A-M-O-N-
D-I-D-N-T-

I finger signed back.

W-H-O-
T-O-L-D-
U-

Jeremy's happy, want to be your friend smile, slid off his face in concentration.

I couldn't help but laugh. Of course a few people knew. Mark had probably leaked info.

Jeremy tried to make it better and finger signed again.

I-
H-A-V-E-
T-A-B-A-C-C-O-
F-O-R-
U-

I started to finger sign back thanks, when the guard in the tower got my attention by tapping on the microphone.

He was turned and completely facing me. Even from 30 yards away and 30 feet in the air it was obvious he was irritated. He announced over the loudspeaker, **"No communicating with the chow hall!"**

I nodded my head and avoided looking at him. The inmates on the yard all turned their attention to me in the corner.

About 70 yards down the asphalt track, the program office door opened. Mark stepped out with a cup of coffee in his hand. He walked 10 feet to the curb at the edge of the track and waited.

A minute later Security Escort Heart and Ligazzaro walked out of the program office.

Mark turned around like he was expecting them. They met in the middle of the track and talked in conspiratorial whispers like convicts. A few seconds later, Mark nodded his head. Heart and Ligazzaro turned and walked toward the main gate to D yard. At that fence, Heart opened it with a key and they disappeared from view on their way toward the other three yards, Solitary or the main control and hospital.

Mark turned back and noticed me in the corner. I waved him over.

On the yard, if you had a spot to post up and study, inmates were differentiated by size and body language from a distance. In Mark's case, at well over six feet tall, his big, round, baldhead, with reading glasses perched on his forehead, stood out even though he was dressed like everyone else. His furtive glances and posture also separated him from the others. His walk was normal.

On his way to me, I studied the rest of the yard. Past Mark down the track to the left, it bended around a corner in front of building 5 where our only table was. Six inmates sat on the cement table and many more stood around it.

I noticed Traveler standing larger than the rest shaking hands with other inmates. Built like a giant, the inmates seemed attracted to him like a magnet. He was one of the best people to be around in a riot or war situation.

Unlike most, Traveler had hair. It was short and blond in a crew cut over a chiseled and handsome face. His body was long and muscled without an ounce of fat. In his mid 30's now, he'd been in and out of juvenile hall and prison for nearly two decades for drug and poverty related crimes.

Rocky was standing shoulder to shoulder with him. He was a pit bull of a man at 6 feet tall, but stocky and full of bunched up powerful muscles and over 240 pounds, without any fat. He was so blocky, he looked nearly invincible, like he could withstand blows from a baseball bat, and probably had. His eyes were beady, he had a gap in between his front teeth, and he looked rabid. He also always stood squared off with almost everyone as if he was constantly on guard and sizing up the situation for the absolute best position to strike from. Rocky loved Traveler because they were both heroes in a riot with the Mexicans on A yard where they held off over a dozen Mexicans and beat a number of them down. In the all out riot, the rest of the 60 something White inmates on the yard, got pummeled ruthlessly by over 400 Mexicans.

Standing next to Rocky was Gary and Horse. Gary was just over 50 years old and the elder from San Bernardino, the meatiest section of the Inland Empire, known as the I.E, one of the biggest groups of inmates in all of California. Gary was bald, not by choice, but exceedingly hairy over his very strong body at just over 6 feet tall and 210 pounds. Horse, was also from San Bernardino, an integral relative to the Hell's Angels and also considered an elder. He was short at less than 6 feet and had an average build, with thick brown hair and a welcoming smile.

A few other White inmates walked away from the table toward the handball court bouncing a ball.

Toward me, Mark was walking the track underneath the guard in the tower and stopped to talk to a few White inmates working out.

They were standing at the edge of the asphalt track waiting in line to do a set of pull-ups. There was vigilance in the way they were standing, like soldiers holding down a spot in the 4th row of bars. Past them, nobody was working out in the last two rows of bars going that direction.

The 5th set of bars, closer to me, had a line of Asian inmates waiting for a set. The 6th set of bars also had a line of Asians. But the last two rows of bars were empty.

Mark finished talking to the White inmates and walked the last 20 yards to me in the corner.

The guard in the tower watched him all the way.

I shook Mark's hand and asked, "Are those White inmates holding down that 4th row of bars for a reason?"

Mark nodded his head and said, "Yep. The Asians were talking about using it."

That was not supposed to happen. Every inch of the yard was divided. When the prison was built and opened, wars had established exact territories between races and gangs. The toilets, showers, drinking fountains, tables, courts and every other inch of space had been determined years ago. To cross those lines was the ultimate form of disrespect.

I said, "I'll get to the bottom of it. I know the Asian Shot caller."

Mark always wanted to be in the know. He nodded his head and said, "You're talking about K-9."

I nodded and said, "Yep. The Blacks might be putting pressure on them."

Mark didn't look like he understood. I helped him.

"The Black inmates are at absolute war with the Mexicans for giving them a beat down, twice now. They know the Mexicans are coming after them. They might be trying to stir the pot by having the Asians penetrate space on the yard that we share with the Mexicans."

Mark's expression changed to understanding and his lips clamped down in concentration. He said, "I get it. If we don't hold them off, the Mexicans get mad at us."

I said, "Yep. We are the much easier war only having 8% of the yard population because they are evenly matched numbers wise."

Mark looked toward Building 1 and I wondered what information he had from Heart and

Ligazzaro. He told me. "Things are heating up. They're going to try to let them off lockdown."

That didn't make sense. After the incident in 3 Building where the tower guard intentionally opened the wrong cells for the showers, and a mini riot ensued, this was not the time to try.

Then it hit me. Prison guard Gomez and his crew knew this was coming and that intentional mistake was either to try and stop it, or a way to ensure that letting the two warring races come off lockdown wouldn't work.

I asked, "Is that what Heart told you?"

Mark nodded his head and said, "Yep, the Warden is getting pressure to let them off lockdown since it's been 6 months already."

Mark looked like he had ants in his pants. He kept looking at our Building and I pictured him on the side of Boxer's cell like a coat rack talking about the issue. Being that close to the heart beat of the yard was addicting for him.

I asked, "Before they let us off lockdown did they search this yard for weapons?"

If they didn't, the yard would go on complete lockdown again for the search.

Mark nodded his head and said, "Yep but they didn't dig any holes, and they just used metal detectors."

I asked, "Did they search the chow hall and laundry?"

Mark nodded his head and said, "Yep... I have to go tell Boxer what's going on."

He turned to go and I asked, "Where do I go to start my new barber job?"

Mark turned back and smiled like he just remembered he'd gotten me the job. He walked a couple steps back to me and looked down the track. He said, "You see that guard walking by the Program Office?"

There were two guards walking that I recognized from being on the yard for a few days handling business prior to the lockdown.

Both were Mexican. One looked like the leader. He had slightly bowed legs and carried himself like he'd been in the military for an extended period. He was just less than 6 feet tall, had a light complexion for a Mexican and had incredibly perceptive eyes. His yard guard partner stood out from him because he looked less aware. He was a darker, blockier Mexican who looked like he could have easily been a prisoner. Both gave off the impression that they were compassionate to inmates rather than disdainful.

Mark said, "You should go check in with them right now and get your barber box."

Chapter 19

A Barber That Doesn't Cut Hair

This was a bold step. As I walked the track I felt my fear dissipate. It was replaced with confidence that I was able to handle it, as long as I continued to never hesitate to trust my instincts.

The guard in the tower was staring at the inmates 30 feet below him working out on the bars and noticed me walking.

The gym was directly under him and stuffed to maximum capacity with inmates. It looked like a horrible nightmare. Rows of triple rack bunk beds filled a space the size of a basketball court. Inmates were packed in crowds and standing at the doors looking through the windows like sardines.

I briefly studied the Black and Asian inmates and felt the tension. They had to find ways to get along and share 8 showers and 8 toilets between 140 inmates.

During regular times, when there wasn't an ongoing race war segregating the inmates, and all the races were inside, it was so regulated that certain rows in between the triple bunks were for the White and Mexican inmates and others were for the Black and Asian inmates.

The yard guards were 20 yards away, just past the canteen and laundry, and the lead guard was inserting a huge skeleton key the size of a small gun into a door.

I sped up my pace and that got their attention.

I held up my right hand and changed my posture and expression as I slowed down to give them space, to show that I wasn't coming to assault them.

Five feet away I positioned myself a respectful distance and said, "I'm the new White barber."

The veteran lead guard who looked ex military took the initiative and asked, "Have you been a barber before?"

I realized he was sizing me up and answered, "No."

He asked, "Were you a barber on the streets?"

I said, "Nope."

He asked, "Have you cut people's hair before?"

I finally understood the line of questions. He was trying to determine my motivations. Barbers, who didn't do it as a trade, did it to hustle drugs and weapons. Or, the shot caller used the Barber as a torpedo to get to any building to stab someone if necessary.

I said, "Never."

He asked, "Why are you the White Barber then?"

I said, "So I can get out of my cell anytime."

Both guards smiled at me. The younger guard actually laughed and said, "At least he's honest."

The lead guard had a nameplate on his chest on the right side, P. Torrez. The rest of his uniform was standard issue green fatigues. Like a soldier, he had his pants tied under his pronounced boots that came to mid calf and on the bottom had rubberized spikes.

The younger guard's nameplate read, J. Jimenez. His fatigues were normal and a little sloppy over cheap black shoes.

I took back the initiative and asked, "What do I call you, Torrez? Do I check in here to get the box? How do I do this?"

Torrez said, "You can call me Torrez or C.O. Torrez. Same thing for my partner Jimenez."

I asked, "Were you ever in the military?"

The two guards looked at each other. It was hard to read them.

Torrez nodded his head and asked, "How did you know? Were you in the military?"

I shook my head, "Nope. I can just tell."

The military wasn't all that different from being in prison in a way. They were housed in barracks and had to get along with other men in crowded situations. The alpha dog tendencies were also the same. Prolonged service in those conditions bred a certain posture that never went away.

I asked, "See any wars?"

Torrez nodded his head yes and then surprised me. "I was in the Mexican Military for almost 20 years until the P.R.I. lost the election."

I couldn't help but ask, "Did you escort any massive loads of drugs across the border for the Sinaloa Cartel? Was that stuff true I read in the papers?"

The LA Times had reported that a convoy of Military dressed soldiers escorted a billion dollar drug load across the border.

Torrez didn't answer and took back the initiative and said, "Come on. Lets get your box and I'll tell you how this works."

They walked inside, wary of me behind them, and immediately took an angle to view me.

On the ground in the corner, were three black boxes, next to a couple of basketballs and other equipment.

Torrez squatted down and examined the boxes until he found one with a W inscribed in the corner. He picked it up and set it in front of me.

He said, "Open it."

I squatted down. The box was just like a standard toolbox. I unlatched it, opened it and looked up at Torrez.

He said, "You check in with me as soon as yard opens. You're supposed to turn in the box everyday but I don't make you, except on Friday's for the weekend. That means you can keep it in your cell a lot."

I nodded my head and waited.

He said, "Take everything out and examine it to make sure you have everything."

Inside there was a plastic shelf just like a toolbox that held the clippers, a cleaning kit and all the different sized guards. I lifted the shelf. Underneath there was a black plastic cover. I lifted it and found a plastic bottle of oil and some more cleaning tools.

Torrez said, "Take it all out and make sure it's accounted for."

While I looked at it Torrez kept talking.

"You will go to each building whenever you want and if they let you in they let you in, if they don't, try later. When they do, walk straight to the podium to check in with the building guard. The building guard might go through your box like you are now. Your box is subject to search at anytime so never put your drugs or weapons in it."

I looked up to see if they were smiling. Both had dead serious poker faces.

I said, "I didn't get this job to smuggle with."

Prison guard Jimenez said, "The White Barber doesn't last that long on this yard..."

He went on to tell me about the last three White Barbers. The last one, Blitze, a well-known Skin Head from Venice Beach, used the Barber box to get into Building 5 to get into a fight right in front our cell the second day we arrived at the prison with an inmate I knew. The White Barber before Blitze was a heroin addict doing a life sentence who stabbed a Mexican dealer in the neck in Building 2 that eventually caused a massive riot on the yard that sent over a dozen White inmates off the yard on stretchers. The White Barber before that ran up a thousand dollar drug debt for heroin and meth, before abandoning the yard like a coward, leaving the rest of the White inmates to deal with the angry Mexicans.

I finished putting everything back in the box, stood up and said, "I know the history."

Torrez nodded his head and waited me out. I didn't say anything.

He said, "All I ask is for you to be honest with me."

I said, "I'm straight up, but don't talk much."

Torrez nodded his head in a manner that said we were finished. I picked up the box and walked ahead of them.

Back on the asphalt track I hesitated for a second and then walked back to my corner spot.

On the way I stopped in front of the gym and set my box down.

The guard in the tower 30 feet above me said, "Don't put your box there."

It was out of his view, directly under him. It was also inside a red square that was off limits because of its close proximity to the gym doors.

The box was already a pain in the ass. I grabbed it and set it sideways in the 4th row of pull-up bars.

There were still two inmates working out, both Skin Heads.

I nodded my head and said, "I'm BJ."

The younger Skin Head said, "I know. I'm Casper from O.C.S."

I asked, "Are you like the friendly ghost?"

The question irritated him. He was trying so hard it was hard not to mess with him.

He was only 20 years old and was already a career criminal. Raised in Anaheim, near Angel's Stadium, he never had a chance. His mom was a meth addict and the local drug addict community raised him.

I shook his hand right as he asked, "Why'd they take Damon and not you?"

That sentiment had to be coming from Hitler.

I said, "Because he cut his finger, and was the closest to the scene."

The other Skin Head stretched out his hand and said, "Thanks for doing the yard a service."

I shook his hand and said, "Thank you. Who are you?"

He said, "Tommy Gun."

Tommy Gun was in his late 30's and was also from Orange County. He was a big meth dealer on the streets and well known. I'd heard a lot about him over the years, but never met him until now.

After 10 sets of pull-ups, I asked, "Where's Hitler? Why didn't he come to yard?"

Hitler is a high-powered Skin Head, who was sent to this yard from Calipatria where he stabbed a White inmate for the Aryan Brotherhood. It was a legit stabbing over a drug debt out on the yard. It gave him status. I loved him because he was a soldier, but didn't like his style. His brand of Skin Head was 14/88 full of hate. He was of the ilk that thought that the more hate he held, the cooler and better Skin Head he was. It got to the point where he held so much disdain for those around them, that his face took on a look that was so far past cynical, that it radiated from his posture and facial expression as if there were always a putrid odor around. This perpetual state of being offended, offended me every time.

Casper's expression said a lot. He knew. He waffled and said, "I don't know why he didn't come out. He must have a good reason since its mandatory yard."

I understood. He was rebelling that I was the White shot caller and that Damon was gone. It was his way of saying that he didn't approve of me. He was challenging me. He was undermining me."

Tommy Boy said, "He must be sick or something."

I nodded my head and said, "I'll go check on him."

Chapter 20

Straight Hate 14/88

Building 5 was 70 yards down the track. On the right, I passed the canteen, laundry and Program Office before the straight away part of the track ended. Then on the right, the main gate to D Yard had razor wire in circles running both ways. In the corner perched facing the yard was an old video camera. I already determined it was worthless and just for show. Mark said there had never been video evidence used in court and there had been literally hundreds of stabbings and fights. It didn't even cover more than 40% of the yard from its angle anyway. However, it was still a big part of the reason why I posted up in the opposite corner, completely out of view.

The track turned that part of the quarter mile loop and Building 5 sat in the corner. I walked off the asphalt track onto a thin cement path that led to the heavy steel green door vestibule.

Above, a square of bulletproof tinted window was empty from the shadow of a guard.

To the side of the vestibule door, there was a metal handle next to a button to alert the guards of an arrival. The button was for the guards; the handle was for the inmates.

I rattled the handle.

Through the intercom next to the handle and button I heard static filled, "Yes. What do you want?"

I said, "I'm the White Barber. I want to check on someone."

Less than a minute later, a guard's shadow showed up above. He stuck a block gun out one of the portals facing down in my vicinity.

The guard at the tower spoke back into the intercom, "Hold on. I'm asking Gomez if you can come in."

I was betting Gomez would allow it. He was a successful instigator and warmonger because he stayed involved in prison affairs. He was the reason Blizte was able to get in to handle his mission. Gomez was already aware of a controversy brewing. Now he would want to know who the new White Barber was.

We had trouble with Gomez our first day. He told a Black inmate who asked when the lockdown was going to end that it would take years. In response to why, he said because the Mexicans would respond. In response to a number of Black inmates yelling at him to stop stirring the pot, he yelled not to be mad at him, to be mad at the White inmates who never stayed on lock down long. I had responded that he should shut up as a fat guard who only had to know how to count to two to get the job. Gomez had threatened us that he could have us shot by a number of tower guards he controlled.

This was going to have shock value entertainment to see his face as the Barber.

The vestibule door rattled and shrieked open for 5 long seconds in response.

I entered the tunnel looking straight ahead but still noticed the guard above with the block gun walking at the same pace over a clear thick window.

Half way through the tunnel Gomez came into view sitting at the podium 15 feet into the building.

He smiled, as if this life was a bowl of experiences he could manipulate and enjoy.

He said, "BJ come here."

I stopped at the podium and felt my face unable to stay stoic. A smile broke through and I said, "Good to see you again."

He asked, "Who you here for?"

I said, "That big inmate in cell 207."

Gomez said, "Oh inmate Miller, I mean Hitler to you inmates."

How did he know his AKA? Either because Hitler was loose with it, or he heard other inmates using it, or it was on file and he researched it.

I looked up at Hitler's cell. He was standing at the door.

Gomez said, "Empty your box in front of me."

I squatted on the ground and pulled everything out.

Gomez said, "Put it back. I'm allowing you five minutes to discuss White business."

On the way to the stairs, a number of Black and Mexican inmates yelled out of their cells.

One yelled, "*Hey Barber! Can you come here for a minute?*"

Another one, "*Hey Wood! Can you take this to cell 230?*"

I felt bad for them. They were all on lockdown and stuck. But on the other hand, they might as well spend their day stuck in slow motion by using their fishing lines to transport their own messages rather than give me trouble with Gomez my first day on the job.

I didn't even look at any of the cells and climbed the stairs. At the top I glanced at Hitler's cell. He was posted at the door.

Hitler stood at well over 6 feet and filled up the view of his cell. He had his head cocked at an offended angle. His face looked hesitant.

I set my box down and positioned my back to the wall facing the gun tower. At the side of each cell there was an inch of space. I leaned close and asked quietly, "Why didn't you come to yard? Did Gomez keep you inside?"

Hitler didn't say anything for a second. He must not have expected me to be able to check on him so fast. Was he going to make up something weird?

Finally he said, "I just didn't feel like coming out."

I said, "That isn't a good example to set. A lot of people look up to you. Why you doin this?"

He didn't say anything again. I pivoted 180 degrees to look at him. His face was resolute like he was being challenged.

I was guessing that he had gotten in touch with all the Skin Heads on the yard in messages to take over as their leader now that Damon was gone. The way Casper was acting was part of my proof.

Instead of answering, Hitler asked, "Why'd they take Damon and not you?"

I felt my anger boiling over and it mixed with frustration that Damon was gone for a while. I scrunched up to the side of the cell and said, "Check this out Hitler I'm sick of you questioning me. Do you have a problem you want to handle?"

It felt good to go on the offensive. I would rather deal with all my pent up frustration, than let it boil further.

Hitler backed off and said, "Calm down. I just asked you why they took Damon."

I hammered him with the truth as I was reading it. "No you didn't. You insinuated I handled the whacking wrong rather than appreciating the risk me and my homeboy took for the entire yard."

Hitler either misread me, or he wasn't used to being called out so fast. He said, "That isn't how it is...I'm just pissed that Damon is gone."

I said, "You're no where near as pissed as me. That's my other half in here. He's also like a brother to me on the streets."

I pivoted to look at Hitler again. He was nodding his head like he understood. He realized I didn't care if I stayed on the yard or not.

He said, "You miss him huh?"

I got up to the side of the cell door feeling better. Maybe I nipped a potential problem in the bud. I said, "Hell yeah I miss him. But I'm getting him back on this yard."

Chapter 21

Divided You Fall

The next day on the yard it got worse. I was in my corner doing pushups watching everything.

Hitler came to the yard on a mission. He avoided me and corralled all the Skin Heads. One by one, he gathered them coming out of each building. He and 14 other Skin Heads walked to the White table where Gary, Horse, Rocky and Traveler were.

Hitler tried to scoop up Traveler with him and failed. Even from over 100 yards away I could feel their tension. Hitler stood at an angle like he was challenging Traveler. Traveler brushed him off like he wasn't interested.

Hitler overreacted in an offended way and waved his crew with him into the interior of the yard. About 30 yards away from the White table he organized all 15 of them in a circle.

It was obvious. It was a circle of White Supremacy Skin Heads who thought they were better than everyone else. If you weren't in the circle, you were beneath them.

Isolators. Dividers. Chaos creators.

The rest of the White inmates nearby started to notice and one by one formed a group around Gary, Horse and Traveler.

They all congregated on or around the table facing Hitler's group as if they were trying to understand.

Some were shaking their heads like they did understand.

The White inmates were now broken into two distinct groups.

The guard in the tower was watching everything.

I knew if I walked there I wouldn't be able to control my temper so I stayed put and worked out.

Gary, Horse and Traveler got up from the table and walked the asphalt track.

I did another two sets of pushups before they got to me.

Gary looked slightly amused. Horse was studying me. Traveler looked preoccupied. Rocky looked exceedingly angry and stood off to the side, in his always squared off position. He said, "I've seen this happen on other yards. I'm telling you, Hitler is going to cause problems."

I finally said something, "We already have our hands full of problems. The Blacks are telling the Asians to use our pull up bars."

Everyone looked over there. With the problem Hitler was creating, none of the White inmates were using the pull up bars.

Three Asian inmates were using our 4th bar we shared with the Mexicans.

Gary asked, "What do you want to do?"

I was glad we had a major problem. The risk of a riot in prison either forced unity, or further disintegration. Either way, it forced a resolution. I said, "Lets go kick em off the bars and get all the Whites to hold them down while I talk to the Asian shot caller."

Everyone nodded their head but waited for me to take the first step. Now that we had direction and I had momentum behind me, I walked.

Having such strong men following me lifted my spirits.

There were over a dozen Asian inmates using the pull up bars.

The first line of bars had three Asians in line. The second line of bars had four Asians in line. The third line of bars had another four Asians in line.

That's where it should have stopped. Instead, there were another three Asians using the next line of bars that we shared with the Mexicans.

In the gym 20 feet away, a line of Black inmates were watching.

We stopped in a circle surrounding the Asians using our bar. The three Asians avoided looking at us and continued to face the pull up bar. I stepped forward a few feet and said in irritation, "What are you doing on our workout equipment? Where's K 9? I need to talk to him about this crap."

One by one, the Asian inmates using each row of pull up bars turned and stared at us. None of them said anything. They were all waiting for someone else to deal with it.

In the silence I spoke up again, "You guys have to stay on your bars. Move over."

I motioned my hand over and stepped in closer to the three Asians. The rest of the White inmates stepped in with me.

The three Asians moved to the next line of Asians.

The yard got instantly more quiet and watchful.

The rest of the Asians on the yard, about 70 in number, were at the handball court directly across the yard from us about 40 yards away. Except for the four on the court, they were all turned our way, discreetly watching.

The only inmates unaware were the Skin Heads in the circle.

One of the Asians said, "K 9 at da handball court. Want me to get him?"

I nodded my head and said, "Yeah."

Everyone on the yard was silent and looking at us. Even the circle of Skin Heads was starting to become aware. One by one, their heads turned to look.

The guard in the tower above us was staring at us holding a block gun pointed downward.

To break up the tension, I walked to the pull up bar in our 4th row. I had so much anxious energy mixed with adrenaline that I did over 30 pull-ups.

The rest of the White inmates formed a line. I passed Traveler on my way to the back of the line and he said, "Show off."

At over 240 pounds of muscle, Rocky was able to do nine pull-ups but he had to cheat a few by using his legs to swing his body up the last half of his reps. Still, it was a mammoth feat.

Gary followed him and did a set of 10 perfect pull-ups.

Horse, wearing a blue bandanna wrapped around his neck like an outlaw, only did three pull-ups.

Traveler was next, and he did 14 pull-ups, but looked the most dangerous with such a long wingspan and able frame at over 220 pounds.

I waited to do my set and the rest of the men gathered around me to watch the yard.

The White inmates who were sitting on the table watching the circle of Skin Heads were getting up as a group. They noticed what was happening and were on their way.

The Asian that went to talk to K 9 was mixed into the group of Asian's at the handball court. K 9's short body was somewhere in the group.

We watched the group of White inmates walk past the circle of Skin Heads on their way to us.

I looked up at the guard in the tower. He was watching and speaking into his microphone on his shoulder. He was briefing other guards.

In each Building on the yard, a guard in the tower became visible as a shadow through the tinted bulletproof window. A block gun hung out a few windows pointed at the ground.

I mentioned under my breath, "That guard up there just notified everyone of a potential riot."

Rocky said, "It feels like that movie Brave Heart."

Instead of talking directly underneath the guard in the tower to the White inmates who were arriving, I waved our group with me and walked toward them.

I ushered everyone into the yard another 10 yards and spoke just loud enough for everyone to hear. "I'm taking Traveler, Gary and Rocky with me to the Asians. The rest of you go get the Skin Heads ready in case this pops."

Gary asked, "What about the bars? Don't you want a few Whites holding them down so the Asians don't use them?"

I had changed my mind on the fly. "Nope. We are going to force K 9 to deal with it."

On the way across the yard to the handball courts Horse said to me, "You want k 9 to order it so he doesn't look bad huh."

I said, "Yep. If we order them off it makes him look weaker."

The handball courts consisted of one wall that was 30 feet high. The White and Mexican inmates shared one side and the Asian and Black inmates shared the other side.

Almost all the Asian inmates on the entire yard, about 70 of them, had come to their side of the handball court like a magnet. The collection of inmates stood on the curb next to the asphalt track and in a semi circle into the yard around their side of the court.

I stopped 20 feet away with Gary, Horse and Traveler and waited facing them.

Nothing happened. All the Asians stared at us in anticipation. Even the four Asians on the handball court, in the middle of a game, stopped and faced us.

Twenty yards to our right, the circle of Skin Heads got up and inched closer.

The tension on the yard magnified and got even quieter. The only thing you could hear was your own heartbeat thumping with adrenaline.

One of the Asians standing at the curb maneuvered something in his back pocket.

Another Asian next to him squatted down and used his hand to unbury a weapon along the curb.

I broke the tension by walking a couple steps toward the Asian enclave. Each step was a penetration into their space. I asked, "***k 9! Can I speak to you? This is BJ!***"

I was letting all of them know my position for the White inmates and putting K 9's status as the shot caller for the Asians out in the open as well.

K 9 moved from the curb at the edge of their side where the handball wall was. He was positioned in the blind spot from the main tower guard.

Behind me I heard Traveler say, "Keep your eyes on those two Asians on the curb to the left, they have shanks."

K 9 walked through the handball court toward me. I stayed right where I was, five feet away from their court, already in space that was theirs.

K 9 looked around 40 years old, but could have been as old as 50. He was a soldier. Every inch of his 5'7 short stout frame was full of explosive muscle and his body radiated leadership. It was

117

evident in the way he was standing like a ruler a few feet from me. He nodded his head and a little smile broke through his otherwise stoic face. Then he stepped closer and reached out his hand and said, "BJ."

I shook his hand and said, "We have an issue to work out."

There was an Asian saying that I lived by, that a crisis is the best time to find and seize an opportunity. I needed K 9 to see the same thing.

K 9's smile disappeared and was replaced with an indifferent stoic granite mask. Even though he was shorter than me, he wasn't giving up any ground. He took control of the situation by pivoting and waving me to follow him.

I was hesitant for only a moment. He was waving me into territory that belonged to them and the Black inmates.

To be in their space was such a violation, you could get stabbed or cause a riot over it.

I shook off the offense and walked with him across the cement court.

Inmates on the court and nearby parted for us to have a clear path. One step ahead of me, K 9 got to the curb and pivoted 180 degrees. I did the same thing.

K 9 said, "This is my spot to post up."

It was another ideal spot on the yard. The wall impeded the tower guard's view. To the right you could see every part of the yard, including my corner spot. To the left you could see every part of the yard also.

Impressed, I said, "I like it."

K 9's face went from granite stoic to a slight smile. He said, "You have good spot in corner."

K 9 was wearing the most expensive Nike shoes and grey shorts the prison allowed from vendors. He also had an expensive watch and a red bandanna around his neck. It circled a half-inch above his tattoos. His body was a collage of Asian prison art from his neck down. Asian symbols were perfectly placed with scenes of war and gangsters everywhere. It was impressive.

I knew K 9 was an Asian gangster, but was unsure of how much prison life experience he had.

I tested the waters and said, "You know it is better to have this yard to ourselves. We have so much more opportunity to use these courts, the workout bars and the track."

K 9 nodded his head and waited.

I continued, "This war between the Blacks and Mexicans will last a couple more years if we don't get in the way."

K 9 nodded his head and asked, "What u mean?"

I said, "I've been through this many times. Have the Black inmates asked you and your people to bury weapons on the yard?"

K 9's face-hardened into a tighter mask.

I asked, "Did they ask you to use our workout bars?"

K 9 was a statue and I could feel his discomfort.

I went to easier ground and said, "It has happened to me in the past. In the end I felt used."

K 9 reached into his pocket and pulled out two cigarettes. He squatted down and handed me one.

I squatted down with him and watched him light his smoke. He had a battery built lighter that turned orange and slowly ignited his smoke. He put it close enough for me to light my smoke also.

I blew out a cloud of smoke and used my other hand to wave it away lest it rise and be noticeable.

K 9 did the same thing and waited me out.

I said, "I will tell you how I'm doing it. If the Mexicans ask me to help them in a war with the Blacks I will tell them that the only way the Whites get involved is if our space we share is attacked."

K 9 nodded his head and finally said something. "U mean if they rush our side inside of building or our side out here?"

I nodded my head and said, "Exactly."

I could see K 9's brain working. He was seeing my solution as a way to maintain honor and not get used.

I said, "The Black and Mexican inmates are evenly matched. There will be over 400 of each of them out here with us, where as we have much less than 100 each."

K 9 nodded his head and took another puff from his smoke.

I said, "I don't let my people smuggle weapons for them either because those same weapons could later be used on us."

K 9 nodded his head and said, "No weapon help."

I smiled and said, "I look out for the Mexicans because we are allied with them. That means I make sure they aren't hungry while locked down. I pass messages for them. But I don't get in their crossfire."

K 9 nodded his head and his expression changed into a decision. He said, "I tell my people not to take sides."

I nodded my head and said, "I come to you with this after I told a few Asians to get off our work out bars. I realize it is better to talk to you than tell your people what to do."

K 9 nodded his head in understanding and he said, "I make sure that doesn't happen again."

I stood up and shook his hand and nodded my head respectfully.

This time I didn't walk through their court. I walked a few steps to my left and walked through our side of the court.

Gary, Horse and Traveler greeted me to find out what happened. While I told them, other White inmates gathered around. The circle of Skin Heads broke apart and some of them came in to listen.

Hitler's face wrinkled up like a prune in obvious distaste. He reluctantly walked closer.

Right as I finished explaining he said, "You shouldn't have walked through their court."

Traveler turned around and said, "Hitler let me talk to you for a second."

I held my anger in. My adrenaline had already sky rocketed and dropped. Now I was mellow and taking it all in.

The guard in the tower was staring with his block gun in his hand and his head slightly turned to talk into the microphone on his shoulder.

Everyone nearby heard Traveler's voice take on an irritated tone. "Hitler stop causing problems on this yard."

Equally irritated, Hitler said, "I don't like the way this yard is being run."

Traveler said, "Then raise your hand to go on a mission before you divide the yard any further."

Chapter 22

More California Racial Problems

Inmate Danchuck was a White guy from Philadelphia. He was a regular Joe, who went by the AKA, *Phili*. He had a brown mop of hair, brown eyes and didn't come close to fitting into California prison inmate politics, nor did he want to. It cost him.

He was doing a life sentence for murder and had already served over 10 years. At first he worked in the kitchen serving food to the 1,140 inmates on D Yard, until it became too much work mixed with too much politics.

In the kitchen there were Jim Crow policies set up. There were rules like, you can only eat sitting at tables with White or Mexican inmates. There were other space designations, like half the chow hall was only for the Black and Asian inmates to work out in during breaks. At the end of each shift, the extra food for each race was divided perfectly, but at times that process caused tension. The real pressure came with dividing the syrups, jellies and juices, all of which inmates sold to make wine. *Phili* couldn't handle the heat, so he got out of the kitchen.

With the Black and Mexican inmates on an extended lockdown, a lot of other jobs were open for the taking.

Phili decided he wanted to work in Laundry.

Working in laundry had similarities and different difficulties. Many of the inmates wanted the best possible state clothes and shoes to look as sharp as possible for visits with family members or future loved ones. It was also a status symbol to be dressed in brand new blues with creases so sharp they could draw blood.

Another hot item out of the laundry were the shoes. Occasionally, there were brand new boots to be had with extra black rubber soles and spikes that looked sharp contrasting with the brown leather. Not to mention the stomping ability in a fight or riot.

With 80% of the yard on lockdown, once a week, the laundry workers brought clothes into the buildings and gym for exchange.

Phili worked with an Asian inmate named Liu and they both answered to the free staff laundry boss named Don.

Don had both *Phili* and Liu organize enough pants, shirts, boxers, socks and shoes for their trip to the buildings. Everything was going fine, until building 3.

Like normal, on the way in the vestibule everyone heard the guard in the tower tap the microphone for an announcement. "**Attention in the Building! Laundry exchange!**"

As soon as *Phili*, Liu and Don entered, inmates from cells yelled out requests to get attention. It was like animals at a pound barking for a new arrival.

"**Hey Phili! Hook me up with some pants for my visit!**"

"**Yo Liu! I need a brand new blue shirt!**"

On and on it went and one request was drowned out by the next one. The noise got so loud almost every word yelled was indistinguishable.

The first cell dumped out the clothes they wanted to exchange and the new clothes were shuffled in.

After a few cells, a Black inmate who knew *Phili* yelled, **"Hey Boy! Yo Phili! Hook a nigger up with some brand new boots!"**

That's where *Phili* blew it. He should have been more discreet in hooking up a Black inmate. With the racial policies, he was supposed to have Liu help him. By helping a Black inmate, that dipped into the help that was supposed to go to a White or Mexican inmate. It was the same for Liu. He wouldn't help the White or Mexicans; he instead would pass the special requests off to *Phili*.

Phili found a brand new pair of boots and placed them in front of the Black inmate's cell.

A young gang banging Mexican a few cells away got *Phili's* attention and waved him to the side of the cell door. He asked quietly, "Hey *Phili* can you hook me up with that brand new shirt right there?"

Phili looked to where the gangbanger was pointing and shook his head no. He came back to the side of the cell and said, "That one is reserved."

Instead of trying to barter for a brand new shirt, the young gang banger who went by Sappo said, "You better take care of us or we're going to regulate you."

Sappo lived in the cell with another young gangbanger from LA who was also serving a life sentence who went by Degas.

Degas said even louder, "You can't keep your job if you get holes poked in you."

The next cell had a couple of young gangbanging Mexicans from Riverside who got into it and yelled, "You better hook us up White boy!"

Another Mexican yelled, "Don't get your square ass in a wreck *Phili*!"

The free staff employee Don was standing a few cells away helping Liu shuffle clothes into a Black cell and heard the commotion. He turned and walked over.

Sappo and Degas were staring death warnings to *Phili*. *Phili* was visibly shaking in anger. He set another set of clothes into their cell and Sappo pushed it back and said, "Those don't fit. I want good ones."

Don stepped in and finished the job and said, "You get what you get."

In the next cell a Mexican said, "When we get off lockdown he's goin to get what he gets."

The building went silent in anticipation. The guard in the tower was holding a block gun and staring. He was talking into his microphone to the guard on the floor at the podium.

Every cell in the building watched in anticipation. As each moment went by the pressure increased.

The guard at the podium came to a decision. He spoke into his microphone and walked toward the cell.

In front of the cell he said, "Come here Don. Let me talk to you."

The building guard walked Don into the office next to the vestibule. A minute later Don's head popped out and he yelled, "Hey *Phili*! Come here!"

Phili was still angry. He did the right thing by not saying anything or staring at the Mexicans. He did the wrong thing by walking to the office and then inside.

One of the Mexicans yelled out, "Hey Sappo and Degas! I bet that White boy is going to tell on you fools!"

Sappo yelled, "That rat will get steel in his neck if he does!"

A couple of minutes later *Phili* walked out of the office, followed by Don and the building guard.

Instead of going back to work, they walked to the podium.

The building remained silent in anticipation. Everyone knew a line had been crossed. For calling *Phili* a rat out in the open, he would have to stab the inmate responsible to maintain honor, or else, it would look like he was a rat.

The vestibule shrieked and rattled open for five long seconds to break the silence. The other tower guard walked with another gun in his hands and got to the window facing the commotion just as a group of other Building guards walked into the building.

Gomez led the procession of guards to the podium. They talked for a couple of minutes and came up with a plan.

Phili stood off to the side. His facial expression changed from angry to uncomfortable. He was scared. Instead of looking at anyone, he averted everyone's attention.

The group of guards, led by Gomez walked from the podium to the cell Sappo and Degas were in.

A few feet away, Gomez pulled out a pair of handcuffs.

The other cell of young Mexican gangbangers nearby yelled, **"I told you Phili would rat!"**

Gomez acknowledged the situation for what it was, another guarantee of violence to look forward to. A smile broke through an otherwise smug expression.

He banged on the cell door with metal handcuffs for added effect and said, **"You know what time it is! Strip down! You're going to sit in the cages while we figure out what to do with you."**

Everyone in the building watched in silence.

Gomez directed the orders:

"Arms in the air!"

"Turn around... Squat down... Grab your ass cheeks and open up... Cough three times... Put your clothes back on... Put your hands behind your back and stick em through the tray slot..."

Sappo's hands inched out of the tray slot in the middle of the cell and Gomez put on the handcuffs.

The next guard did the same thing with Degas.

The cell door popped open.

Both inmates were walked right past *Phili*.

A Mexican from a cell yelled, "**You both will catch extra time on your sentences for this!**"

Another Mexican from another cell yelled, "**You both won't be able to get visits for six months!**"

Chapter 23

Let The Tension Build

It was another scorching hot day in the desert on the border of Mexico. I was in my corner spot on the yard working out and watching everything.

The Black and Mexican inmates were starting to trickle out to the yard in small groups from alternating buildings on different days with the lockdown deescalating. It was starting to fill up already and tension was always high.

Gary, Horse, Rocky and Traveler walked the asphalt track to my left. It was becoming a habit for them to meet and brief me on conditions in their buildings.

After shaking everyone's hands, Gary asked, "What's the deal with *Phili*?"

Boxer, the Mexican Mobster, had put the issue on the ironing board to work on solutions with me. There was one choice for *Phili* to maintain honor, it could be arranged for him to get the chance to do battle inside the Mexican's cell against both of them.

I said, "You know his choice."

With the Mexicans and Blacks at war, everyone understood that this problem with *Phili* was huge. Building 3 had so much tension between the White and Mexican inmates, that neither race was even talking. It was like a bomb, ready to explode into a riot every second of every day.

The tension was starting to leak into other Buildings over it.

Gary said, "That isn't good enough. The Mexicans in our building are starting to act funny."

Rocky had moved Gary into his cell in Building 2 and they were a force on the yard that filled in for Damon as my missing influence.

Rocky said, "You know *Phili* isn't going to man up and go in their cell."

I had talked to Security Escort Heart about the problem. He had talked to the Building guard about our possible solution and got approval to set up the gladiator cell war. All we had to do was set it up.

So far, *Phili* had acted the offended part enough to say he would go in the cell with them, but now that it was a reality, he was balking and saying that it wasn't fair.

Rocky said, "*Phili* had his chance. He's in that sorry ass Building 3 and his time is up."

Traveler didn't say anything. He had been in Orange County Jail with me many times where similar situations came up. It was almost a game, where the young gangbanging Mexicans would put pressure on the White inmates to beat up another White inmate over something they had created, just to avoid a race riot.

Cognizant of being used like that, I wanted to give *Phili* every chance I would want in a similar situation. I said, "*Phili* gets one more option before we have him beat up."

Horse nodded his head in expectation and asked, "What's the run down BJ?"

I said, "He can agree that his hand is in the air for the next hot job for us."

Rocky squared off in his usual way and said, "That's it. Someone go get *Phili*. He's in the batters' box or else."

We all watched Casper and Tommy Gun strolling toward us. Both had shaved heads with racist ink all over them.

Casper had a fresh swastika on his weak looking chest that stood out more prominently than his other artwork that looked like a Mexican had done it.

Tommy Gun was older and more able. He had STRAIGHT HATE 14/88 blasted in ink across his chest and a bunch of other pieces of gravestones mixed in that was obviously done by a White inmate who knew how to tattoo.

The rumor from the Skin Heads was that Hitler was sending Casper on a mission, which put him in the batter's box.

Tommy Gun stopped next to me and asked, "BJ, can I talk to you for a second?"

A few steps away, in hearing of the others, Tommy Gun said, "Hitler wants to know if you want Casper to beat *Phili* up out here on the yard for the Mexicans to see? That way the problem is handled."

The pressure of the yard filling up, along with some noticeable tension with the Mexicans over *Phili*, was causing our White race to tighten up. Though it felt good to unite, I still wanted to see it play out further.

I said, "Tell Hitler I said thanks for the shooter. It might go down that way yet."

Tommy Gun asked, "So what do I tell him, yes or no?"

"No for right now."

Gary, Horse, Rocky and Traveler crowded in around me and we watched Tommy Gun and Casper walk the track past the work out bars.

The pull up bars was full of inmates standing in lines waiting for their turns.

Only about 25% of the Black and Mexican inmates were on the yard and there were still twice as many of them outside compared to the White and Asian inmates.

Rocky squared off like usual and asked, "So what are we doing with *Phili*? I'm sick of this tension with the Mexicans. You know more than half of them are preferring a war with us before they have to face off with the Black inmates."

I nodded my head and said, "We're good with the Mexicans."

Rocky nodded his head and looked across the yard. *Phili* was standing near our White table exercising alone. No other White inmates were associating with him since the problem surfaced. It was one agonizing day after another.

Gary, Horse and Traveler stood at the curb with me and looked there also. Traveler said, "*Phili* would probably beat up Casper anyway."

Everyone laughed and I asked, "Don't we have any other problems in Building 3 for *Phili* to handle?"

Horse said, "Yep. Half that Building doesn't come to yard because they're taking the weak way out and taking medication all day."

I asked, "Do they need the meds?"

Gary said, "A couple of them have been on meds since before I got here but the rest of em jumped on board to get off this yard."

Inmates who told a Doctor they heard voices, or were crazy, built up a file to get $900 in SSI money a month when released from prison for being considered 5150 or legally insane. Prison did make you crazy, but that was the weak way out the back door. It left all the other White inmates in hell fighting an uphill battle being so outnumbered.

I said, "They've all been warned in that building that if they don't have paperwork from another prison to show they were getting meds, they have to stop the process until we decide if they really need the meds or not."

Horse said, "There it is there. *Phili* gets an easy out."

Traveler said what everyone was thinking, "He'll still pee on himself and say it isn't fair."

I said, "He was a killer in Philadelphia but a tame lame with no game in California."

Gary got to the root of the matter, he asked, "How are you so calm over this BJ? What do you have worked out with the head burrito Boxer?"

I said, "He gave me his word that we have all the time we need to deal with *Phili*. I know it feels weird with the Mexicans, but that's just because they're stressed out. They have a lot of fish to fry and one big one."

Traveler said, "The Black war, World War Three for them."

Boxer had told me there was an inmate from Pomona in Building 2 who had his hand raised to stab the Black Crip Shot Caller. That Mexican went by Capone and he just got to the yard after he had deescalated out of the Pelican Bay SHU and then High Desert, an even crazier level 4 prison than this one. To add even more fuel to the gang banging fire, Capone had a prominent tattoo that the Crips were tripping over, CK, for Crip Killer.

Up to this point, I didn't want to tell everyone because if it was well known, and it leaked that it was, it could easily backfire. When that much pressure was being built up, it was best to stay so far away that being unaware was healthy.

Boxer also said that they had some housecleaning to do also. That meant that they had some internal problems that were going to be resolved. Gangbangers, who had dropped the ball at other prisons or on the streets, were about to get stabbed or beat to a pulp, Mexican mafia style.

I decided to share this info with my closest group on the yard. I said, "You can't let what I'm about to tell you get further than right here. The Mexicans are going to go to store for a full month and then start housecleaning. During housecleaning and continued de-escalation, they might rush the Black Crip Shot Caller. All that is to go down before the all out yard riot down the road."

Rocky nodded his head in understanding and said, "That changes everything. No wonder it feels like the Mexicans are tripping, they have their hands full."

Chapter 24

Boxer Time

Boxer had been slammed in a cell for more than 23 hours a day for over five years.

It started when he was sent to the Colorado Super Max facility where there was nothing but Mexican Mobsters, Aryan Brotherhood, notorious terrorists and other high profile killers and gang members. They sat seven floors underground in a double sealed, double barred tomb like cell.

From there, a separate Federal Indictment for Racketeering fell apart and he was sent to Centinella to finish off his other state prison sentence.

Boxer was a few inches shorter than me, but built much the same way, with a compacted frame, full of bunched up muscle that was shredded to the core without any fat. He spoke like a mobster, with a deep voice, but a natural one. There wasn't anything fake about him.

He spoke through the side of his cell; "BJ can you run to Capone's house for me? I got to shoot him this wila." *Mexican Prison slang for a message.*

Up to this point, I wasn't much of a barber. I didn't cut hair. I also resisted being used to pass messages and other errands for people. Once you started doing favors, everyone expected it like the floodgates were wide open.

I said, "Yeah I got you. I have to go to that building anyway."

Boxer changed the subject and said, "Thanks for hooking up my people with chow hall food. Its appreciated big time."

I had organized a White representative in each building to speak for the entire race, much the same way Boxer had it set up for the Mexicans. I had each representative collect a portion of food from the White chow hall workers to pass out to the hungry Mexicans.

Now that they were getting off lockdown, it wasn't necessary.

The guard in the tower tapped the microphone and announced, "**Inmate Fiero, inmate Cuete, inmate Rodriguez, inmate Jackson and inmate Walker get ready for culinary release!**"

Below us cells started popping open. The first part of the de-escalation process was started by allowing Mexican and Black inmates the chance to work in the chow hall and as yard janitors. It had been going on for a couple weeks.

The Warden was also letting more and more Black and Mexican inmates have a chance to go to yard every other day.

The next incentive was a chance to go to store for food and cosmetics. For the last six months, the Black and Mexican inmates had lived off powdered toothpaste and state lye made soap that was given by the guards once a week. A chance to get canned tuna, top ramen soups, beans, cookies and potato chips was also highly desired after only bland chow hall food.

Underneath, a young gangbanger who went by Pyscho met up with two older Mexicans from LA. They all looked as one group to Boxer's cell to check in. It reminded me of a baseball player standing just outside of the batter's box to receive signs for the next play to execute.

Boxer didn't pressure or extort people to my knowledge. He knew how to rally the troops and share what little was available the right way.

He finger signed to all three Mexicans below:

F-I-N-D
O-U-T
N-E-W
A-R-R-I-V-A-L-S
I-N
5
B-L-O-C-K

All three Mexicans read the instructions and nodded. The vestibule grinded and shrieked open and off they went. Behind them were the two Black inmates.

Chapter 25

Capone Isn't Very Friendly

Barber box in hand, I walked through the vestibule on my way to Building 2.

The area in front of our building was territory that the Black inmates controlled. A few feet into the yard past the asphalt track there was a gathering of over a dozen inmates playing dominoes.

The first sign that they were prepared for war was their clothing. These men had been in prison for over 10 years and had package clothing available such as shorts and tank tops. They were wearing state blues top to bottom.

In the 110-degree heat, wearing a blue denim jacket and the same pants was a survival strategy to deter prison knives, gunshots and pepper spray.

Black inmates were only stationed in a 30-yard portion from the corner to their side of the handball court along the curb. They knew the score wasn't settled.

I stopped at the handball court. There was a skinny Black inmate playing with the best Asian handball player.

The Black inmate was a blur. He raced from one end of the court to the other with the agility of a professional athlete.

The Asian was a better handball player, and had been practicing, free from cell confinement during the lockdown. That the game was close was a testament to the Black inmates ability.

He was in shorts and didn't have a shirt on. He didn't seem concerned about a potential attack.

During a heated rally I heard an Asian yell his name, "Tony got game hommie!"

I turned and walked to the vestibule and rattled the handle.

Immediately, a guard above me, already stationed with his block gun pointed out, said, "Yeah. What you want BJ?"

Every building had a tower guard standing at the ready. That wasn't the surprise. Him knowing my name was the shocker.

I said, "I want inside."

He asked, "You cutting hair or just business?"

I said, "Neither. I'm here for social hour."

He snorted a laugh and the vestibule grinded and clanged open. On my way in he said, "Check in with Delgado."

Delgado was at the podium. He was a friend with the building guard in my block. We had watched them walk the yard together for their shifts. Garcia had told me that if I was straight up with him, I could do almost anything.

At the podium Delgado waved me around and I circled to the point I was facing the tower and the White side of the dayroom.

Gary, Horse, Rocky and Traveler were working out with their backs to the wall. Next to them were three Mexicans working out as well. It looked like a military training camp with bodies dropping for pushups in sets of burpies.

After dumping out my entire barber equipment and putting it back, Delgado asked, "Do you need any cells popped open?"

I stood up and shook my head. "Nope. I just need to talk to that inmate in cell 217."

Delgado turned his head to look behind him. We both looked up at Capone. He was standing at the cell door looking like a killer.

He was a dark, short and blocky Mexican who looked around 40 years old. His face was hardened from warfare and void of emotions. His eyes were so penetrating that you felt the energy coming from them like lasers hitting you with some kind of dark intent.

Underneath his right eye, covering his cheek was a tattoo that read CK, in Old English. On his neck there was another stamp of ink signifying his gang in Pomona.

Delgado's face registered a growing understanding that the heaviest business on the yard was underway. He nodded his head, looked away and said, "You only have a few minutes."

Capone knew I was coming. He stared at me with dark brown eyes the entire way.

I set my box down in front of his cell and positioned my back against the wall. In front of me, the guards in the tower were staring at me. Below, Gary, Horse, Rocky, Traveler, and the three Mexicans all took turns glancing at me. Also below, on the other side of the dayroom, Black and Asian inmates looked with less curiosity.

I leaned close to the side of Capone's cell and introduced myself.

Capone said, "Mucho gusto. Can you get into five block for me?"

I said, "Good to meet you also, no."

With a deep guttural voice, Capone asked, "Why not?"

Being in Pelican Bay in the past gave Capone status. However, the prison politics on other yards were more intense in many ways.

While in the Pelican Bay SHU, inmates couldn't get to each other; they never came out of the cell with other inmates. Once released from *the Bay*, the real pressure came with establishing who had the most influence to run the yard. The more inmates who thought they should have the most influence, the more active the deadly activities. Capone was so used to cut throat politics that he was bred into the most evil bully on earth. I could feel it pouring out of him.

After an intense 10 seconds I said, "Cause I don't even run errands for my people. This is a favor for Boxer."

Capone didn't say anything. It got uncomfortable.

I broke first and said, "Plus I don't like the guards in that block."

Capone adjusted his mission and asked, "Can you get a wila in there for me?"

I pivoted 180 degrees to face him and it gave me cover from the guards. I nodded my head that no I couldn't while I pulled out Boxer's wila for him and held it up and then dropped it. With my foot I slid it under his door.

Capone must have known I was done entertaining because he waved me to the side with an irritated, impatient look.

I reluctantly pivoted 180 degrees so my back was to the wall again. I asked, "Uh huh, what?"

He said, "I'll give you some of the dope I get."

I immediately said, "I don't do dope... I got to go. Nice to meet you."

I heard Capone grunt in irritation and didn't look back.

The guards in the tower watched me walk downstairs and one said something to Delgado.

Delgado turned around in his chair to face me and asked, "Are you done in here?"

I asked, "Can I talk to my people over there?"

Delgado nodded and said, "Sure. Just check in with me before you leave in case I decide to search you."

I set the box down on the wall and started working out next to Gary. While they did burpies, I did handstand pushups.

In between sets I studied the tension radiating from cells. Almost every cell had either Black or Mexican inmates with two bodies stuffed together watching everything quietly, too quietly.

In between sets I asked Gary in a whisper, "Which cell is Green Eyes in?"

Gary popped up from the ground after three push-ups in his set of burpies and said, "Cell 213."

Capone was watching us take glances just to the left of his cell. He knew we were checking out Green Eyes.

Green Eyes was a light colored Black Crip with green eyes. He wasn't a big man, or athletic looking. Nor did he radiate intimidating energy. To control the Crips on the yard, he had to be the real deal.

Gary, Horse, Rocky and Traveler finished working out. They surrounded me and shook my hand one by one.

Rocky asked, "Did you hear about all the new arrivals in five block?"

I said, "Nope but I just found out there's dope in there."

Gary said, "Some Mexican who goes by Termite from the Coachella valley brought in a boat load."

Traveler said, "We got a couple of monster Skin Heads in there plus another White dude from B Yard who was in a riot with the Blacks."

Chapter 26

New Arrivals Change Everything

On the way to Building 5 I saw the Black inmate who'd been playing handball. He was running backward, firing punches and bobbing and weaving like a boxer.

I said, "That's quite a routine you got Tony."

Tony stopped and ran in place and asked, "Do I know you hommie?"

I shook my head no and said, "Nope. I saw you playing handball and heard your name. Have a good one."

Tony smiled and returned to his training. He was the only Black inmate roaming the yard. The rest of the Blacks, about 200 of them, were all in the opposite corner watching things.

I rattled the handle and immediately heard the guard in the tower above me ask, "What you want BJ?"

Above, the guard held a rifle in his hands pointed at the ground. I said, "I want to meet the new White inmates."

After a few seconds the vestibule door rattled and shrieked open. The tower guard said, "Go check in with Gomez."

The noise in the building was louder than normal. Mexican inmates were yelling from cell to cell.

I walked through the tunnel and saw Gomez. He looked even more angry than normal.

Behind him, every cell had a pair of bodies scrunched together to watch. The Black inmates were quiet and trying to figure out what the Mexicans were doing.

Some of the Mexican cells had fishing lines from one cell to another. Upstairs, a Mexican cell had a line from a cell downstairs. He was pulling it and a brown lunch bag lifted in the air until it was on the second tier, and then inside his cell.

Before I got to the podium a Mexican yelled out, **"Hey White barber can you come here for a second?"**

Another Mexican yelled, **"Hey White brother can you pass this book to my hommie for me please?"**

Gomez asked, "Who do you want to talk to? Chaos, Bam Bam or Sinner?"

I grunted a laugh and asked, "How do you find out everyone's AKA's so fast?"

Gomez hunched over even more and said, "They're to sloppy with em. As soon as they get here they yell who they are to other inmates. I write it all down."

I nodded my head and asked, "Do you want to look in my box?"

Gomez shook his head no and said, "Not this time. Don't go to any Mexican cells. They're all in trouble with me."

Chaos and Bam Bam were in cell 212 and Sinner was next door in 211. They were all standing at attention watching me.

Mexicans yelled out to me even more, "**Hey wood can you do me a favor please?**"

"**Hey stud pass this to the other side of the building for me por favor?**"

Mark had already filled me in. Chaos was finishing off a 20-year prison sentence. He was from San Bernardino.

Bam Bam was just getting started on a 10-year prison sentence. He was from Riverside.

Sinner was from Fresno.

Chaos was so big he was all I could see at first. I said, "I'm BJ and have this yard for the Whites."

Chaos looked like an athlete at 6'7 and over 250 pounds. He had a gigantic baldhead and huge bright blue eyes. His skin was so pale that his cheeks were pink.

He said, "I've heard of you. Thanks for checking on us. This is my cell brother Bam Bam."

Bam Bam pushed Chaos out of the way. He looked like a gladiator at 6'5 and 210 pounds of shredded stature. Added to the look were the scar remnants of a war that should have killed him. On his left shoulder he'd been cut with a razor to the bone for six inches. The path of scars continued down that arm and then hit his mid section from under his chest down his stomach. The cuts were so deep; they were a half-inch thick and looked like ropes of tendons were protruding. Somehow, the scars just missed his tattoos. From his neck down, he was blasted in art that ended in RIVERSIDE across his stomach.

I asked, "What happened to you brother?"

Bam Bam stood taller. He knew everyone's instant thought was that he looked like a rat or child molester and that the mafia hit men just missed taking his life.

He explained a story similar to mine in that he'd run with the Mexican mafia in prison and on the streets. On the streets, some younger gang bangers felt he stepped all over their toes. He was housed with them in the County Jail and while fighting his case; six of them rushed his cell with razors to exact retribution.

I nodded my head. I believed his story and as always, gave him the benefit of the doubt.

At the level he was involved, the details would surface immediately, with some checking.

I got to the potential heart of the matter and asked, "Do either of you do dope in here?"

Chaos pushed Bam Bam out of the way and said, "No brother. I'm a Skin Head who believes drugs and alcohol bring us down, not lift us up."

Bam Bam was honest. He moved Chaos out of the way and said, "I do dope on the streets but not in here. I do drink but don't come out of my cell drunk."

I ran the rest of the program down and explained the frustration with Hitler.

Bam Bam said, "I heard you were running this yard right and I got your back."

Chaos reassured me even more and said, "I don't divide our race brother, I lift it up and unite it so we have a chance."

I stood taller hearing the two solid warriors back me up. I ended with, "Let me know if you need anything. I can get you moved to my building so we're a wrecking ball together."

Next door, Sinner stood waiting. At around 25 years old, he had short brown hair and brown eyes that studied everything. He was only 5'7 and maybe 160 pounds soaking wet.

I said, "Nice to meet you little brother. You don't have any homeboys from Fresno here but we'll look out for you."

Sinner nodded his head. He was young, but he'd been around. Because of his addiction to meth, he'd already done 7 years in and out of jail and prison.

Sinner grabbed his court paperwork and another stack and slid it through the side of the cell door. He said proudly, "That 144 D is my lockup order for the riot I was just in with the Blacks on B yard."

I checked it out and asked, "What was the riot for?"

Sinner said, "It was over a White Crip."

In California prisons there is such extreme racial loyalty that rules had been in place for over 30 years in regards to White Crips. They are deemed race traitors and it is always an on site war that sparks mayhem.

Sinner said, "He's on his way here. He's already caused a riot on A Yard, then B yard and now he's on C Yard waiting to get cleared for yard."

Chapter 27

The Yard is Filling Up

My corner spot on the yard was getting crowded. Half the Black and Mexican inmates were outside and it was already packed.

Chaos and Bam Bam were to my left and Gary, Traveler, Rocky and Horse were to my right. We were doing burpies using the curb for pushups.

There were over 300 Black inmates posted up in their spot. Rows of Crips and Bloods were stationed on the curb from our building to their side of the handball court. Their concrete tables were filled with Black inmates playing dominoes. All were watchful.

The only Black inmate outside of their section was Tony. He was doing pull ups 20 yards away.

Bam Bam said, "That Black dude is playing Russian roulette with his life."

Everyone watched Tony do his set. He was so wiry and strong; he did pull up dips all in one motion. He yanked his body up the pull up bar like a gymnast so high that his midsection was above the bar and he finished the rep with a dip to his chest before swinging back down.

I said, "He doesn't want to become a gang member so he does his own thing."

Gary said, "He should be wise enough to stay in the crowd with em for health reasons."

Most of the Mexicans were in their territory from their side of the handball court to Building 5. Others were in groups of four walking around and working out.

Traveler asked, "BJ you think they're really going to wait?"

I stopped doing push ups and stood tall doing knees to chest to watch the yard. I said, "Yeah, for a little while longer."

Gary didn't think so. He'd told everyone he thought that the internal housecleaning and other missions were a cover to distract everyone.

Gary said, "I still think it's an Art of War maneuver."

It was possible. Another aspect I was keeping in mind was the flow of dope.

Mark had become the mule after I turned down the job. He was getting dope from Termite and bringing it to Boxer, who was then breaking it into parts to spread out. It was easy to determine who held the most power by where the big chunks were going.

Capone was getting a lot but another Mexican who went by Stomper was getting even more.

Stomper was way up the Mexican Mafia chain but was flying under the radar. He was from Rialto in San Bernardino.

I found him using the pull up bars. He finished his set and glanced at me. Then, like a seasoned gangster, he turned to face his henchmen who were working out with him and in the process glanced at the guard in the tower above.

The guard in the tower was focused on watching the handball court.

I knew Stomper was on his way just before he started walking with two other Mexicans.

I said, "Here comes the next in line."

I didn't mind. When I met him at the side of his cell I mentioned some of my involvement in the meth world at a particular time. Stomper knew who I was by reputation.

Instead of making him walk all the way to us, I met him 10 feet from our corner.

He reached out his hand and said, "BJ thanks for looking out for all the Mexicans while we were locked down."

I nodded my head and said, "Welcome. It's a common courtesy. You all good?"

Stomper nodded his head and said; "I just wanted to get at you about your boy Bam Bam over there."

I was standing where I could see Bam Bam and the rest of the Whites watching.

Stomper continued, "He's at the top of the Riverside food chain. That beef he had in the county jail was the youngster's fault and they're being corrected if you know what I mean."

I looked at Bam Bam studying us closely and gave him a nod and looked back at Stomper and said, "That's what I was betting."

Now that we were finished, Stomper stepped around me and shook the rest of the White's hands. His two little soldiers followed him.

After the greetings, Stomper glanced up at the guard in the tower and said, "I like this spot over here. Enjoy the rest of your day."

They walked back toward the pull up bars.

Down the asphalt track 80 yards the Program Office door opened. Mark walked out with Heart and Ligazzaro.

Gary saw me looking over there and looked also. He said, "There's Boxer's yo-yo."

Mark turned and noticed me. He lifted his arm and smiled. His usually expressive face had an even bigger smile. He walked to us so fast it took less than a minute.

From 15 feet away he said, "Rott is on his way here!"

Below: Bam Bam in 2012 after his release.

Chapter 28

Welcome Back Rott

My brother from another mother was standing tall. Damon, AKA Rott, had added even more muscle from his workouts in Solitary Confinement.

He was dripping sweat from a cell routine. Little drops of perspiration cascaded down his long ripped body and his chest muscles jerked every time he moved. The Ace of Spades on his right pectoral looked like it was being flung as he lifted his arm to hold his cell. He said, "Good to be back. What'd I miss?"

I ran it all down and finished with, "It's been lightweight stuff. We're going to have to deal with *Phili* soon."

Damon nodded his bullet head and asked, "How do you want to handle it?"

All the sudden I didn't want it to be my call, I wanted it to be his. He deserved the say so for a while. I felt selfish for the way I set up the job on the child predator. I had the easy part and it cost my friend.

I said, "Hey brother it's your call. Sorry you had to go to Solitary. Now it's my turn to be your missile."

It felt right to hand off the baton. He deserved to be the shot caller and in control of our destiny for a while.

Damon shook his head and said, "Nope. You're not dropping that on me. I want to look like I have less influence to avoid being labeled. I don't want to be stuck in Solitary forever."

I nodded my head and said, "So you want to go Machiavelli on me? You want to Art of War the rest of you're time from you're back pocket? I'll be you're pocket pinball."

Damon tilted his head back in his fake laugh and gave a Popeye imitation. Then he asked, "Where's *Phili* work now?"

I said, "He's back in the Chow Hall in the morning."

Damon said, "That makes him easy."

There were two White inmates who worked in the Chow Hall in line to beat up *Phili*. Done right, they could get away with it.

I was still pushing the baton in his hand and asked, "Is that a green light?"

Damon said, "It sounds like that's what everyone wants."

I said, "We only have a week or so until we have to start walking to chow. No more breakfast in bed."

Now that the lockdown was ending, the final phase was walking to chow. If that worked, all the Mexican and Black inmates would be let out to full program. We had to have the *Phili* problem done with before then.

Damon asked, "Have they let Boxer out yet?"

So far, it looked like he was on his way to Solitary. I said, "Nope. I'm betting he gets taken any day. Probably right before they release everyone to chow."

Damon nodded his head that he agreed and asked, "What's up with the White Crip? Sinner says we're going to get him soon."

Right then everyone heard an alarm in the distance. The high-pitched scream rose and fell a few times before a guard screamed with intensity, "**EVERYONE DOWN!! GET DOWN!!**"

Damon said, "That's probably him on C Yard right now."

The guard in the tower said something to Gomez and everyone heard, "**C Yard riot in front of the gym! Code 3!**"

The vestibule door shrieked and rattled open. A guard in the tower lowered a block gun. Gomez grabbed it and looked at me. He waved me to the ground and yelled, "**Get down BJ!**"

I sat down and watched him run into the tunnel.

The sounds of war continued. Underneath the sounds of the alarm, we heard bodies running, fighting and yelling.

We heard a guard scream with even more urgency, "**GET DOWN!! GET DOWN!!**"

A block gun exploded, "**BOOM!!**"

The action continued and more block guns exploded. Then we heard the guard scream, "**LIVE ROUNDS COMING NEXT!! GET DOWN**"

The live round ricocheted in the distance, "**PING!**"

I leaned close to Damon through the side of the cell and said, "That sounds like two riots on C Yard."

The extended echo was the proof. If it were on our yard it would be louder and more direct.

Damon said, "I hope Mark can get me moved to your cell before that guy gets here."

I said, "If they stab him on C Yard he'll leave the prison. If it's just a riot he's on his way here in 10 days."

The clock was ticking.

Chapter 29

Full Blast

I woke up and felt the difference. The 4 am sounds of shift change left an electric charge in the air. It started with the vestibule shrieking open in the quiet building. That was followed up with Garcia and another guard walking by every cell to count the inmates. Then there was tension.

I got up to perceive where it was coming from. Garcia was sitting at the podium.

In the tower, three guards were wide-awake and communicating. Usually there were only two who were slumped over, barely awake, waiting for the food carts to come hours later.

They were ready for change and their anticipation was the first charge in the air.

I looked at the cells. Every Mexican cell had activity. Usually only a handful of early birds were up with me.

Only a few Black cells showed movement.

I said, "It's going down today brother."

Damon was used to me being up early. He moaned, sat up and asked, "Why you say that?"

I said, "I can always feel it before I see it."

Damon lowered his long frame from the bunk by stepping on the stainless steel toilet. He stood next to me and watched. A minute later he said, "It's my first day back for yard and here comes World War Three."

A couple hours later we heard the vestibule grind and rattle open. Then, the squeaking from the food carts.

A procession of silver carts entered the building. After all eight were inside, the guards pushing them congregated by the podium.

Garcia looked happy. He knew what was coming. The rest of the guards were quiet and watchful.

They were all usually talkative.

After the food carts were wheeled back out, the only noise was coming from the Black inmates communicating.

A Black Crip downstairs yelled out, "**Hey nigga we must be walking to chow tonight!**"

Other Black inmates yelled from cell to cell.

The Mexican inmates were silent.

Damon said, "I feel my skin crawling."

The tension was so thick; it felt like I was choking.

Yesterday, Boxer had sent us messages that helped us understand things. He and Stomper had drawn cards to see which one of them was going to stay. That meant that their strategy was to keep one Mexican Mafia representative on the yard to run things and the other was going to lead the charge in the yard riot.

So far, that was mostly for show because the prison hadn't let Boxer out for yard. But that could change at anytime.

Another piece of the puzzle that we learned about was the internal housecleaning. Capone had brought a death list from Pelican Bay. The list had the names of Mexican gang bangers who were to be stabbed to death.

While that list was being verified, Capone's name came into question and so did the veracity of the list he'd brought.

He might have created the list on his own to deflect attention from his own death sentence from Pelican Bay.

Every one in the building heard the guard in the tower tap on the microphone to signify an announcement.

He said, "**Get ready for yard release for the top tier! Everyone is coming out! Full release!**"

The Black inmates cheered. Most had been locked in the same cell 24/7 for over six months.

The Mexicans remained quiet.

The sounds of cells popping open started at the end of our row. Our cell popped open and I stepped out.

Boxer was standing at his door. His face had more tension around the eyes. I looked past him and noticed all his belongings were on his bunk.

He waved me to the side of his cell and I pivoted 180 degrees to watch the building and talk through the crack.

Boxer said, "BJ try to get them to open my cell."

It was a desperate attempt. It was meant to show he wanted out to all the other Mexicans.

I lifted my hand in the air and held his cell door with my other hand and yelled, "Tower!"

The guard in the tower was releasing the other side. He was down to the last couple of cells.

I yelled out again, "Tower!"

He turned 180 degrees and looked at me and I yelled, "Can you pop my cell? I forgot something!"

Garcia was watching everything and he said something into the microphone on his shoulder to warn the guard in the tower. The guard in the tower shook his head no.

Garcia got up from his chair. He said, "Good try."

I knocked on Boxer's cell door and walked the tier to catch up with Damon.

At the corner I looked in Sparky's cell. Both of their mattresses were rolled up tight over sheet metal bunks. All of their belongings were also boxed up on their racks. It was to help the guards understand whose belongings they were.

We walked down the stairs slowly. There were so many inmates out that the line to get to the vestibule tunnel reached the podium.

Garcia was studying everything like he was hungry to understand. I crept past him as the line moved. It was inch by inch through thick tension.

Chapter 30

Caught Slippin

We made it through the tunnel into the yard. Every building was releasing at the same time.

Over 800 inmates were in motion to find a spot. The energy was almost overwhelming.

The Black inmates were packed into their space in front of us. They stood in a line along the curb watching everything. Streams of Black

Crip and Blood gang members were walking from the buildings to get there.

The Mexicans were in bunches everywhere. Many were meeting at the handball court. Others were at the pull up bars. Others were walking the track. So far, they weren't showing any signs of war.

Damon said, "Let's go to our corner spot."

Traveler stood tall on the curb waiting for us. Next to him in line were Rocky, Gary, Horse, Chaos and Bam Bam.

All had their shirts off ready to work out. They made room for us to get in the middle.

Rocky said, "It's going to pop."

Traveler asked, "Is today the day BJ?"

I said, "Boxer didn't say but it looks like it."

Gary got to our problem. He asked, "What're we going to do about *Phili* now?"

This was the morning *Phili* was going to get dealt with. A couple of youngsters were on board to beat him up."

I looked behind us to the chow hall and saw them.

I said, "Tell them to hold off for a few minutes. I want to get at Stomper first."

If we gave them a green light it could cause the riot between the Mexicans and Blacks to kick off spontaneously.

If today were the day, the Mexicans would all charge as one as soon as the alarm sounded.

Gary turned and faced the chow hall and used his fingers to sign:

H-O-L-D
O-F-F
F-O-R
A
M-I-N-U-T-E

Stomper was at the pull up bars watching everything. On cue, he turned his head and looked at me.

I nodded and looked at the guard in the tower. He was busy looking at the handball courts. I finger signed:

I
N-E-E-D
T-O
T-A-L-K

Stomper and his two henchmen walked toward me. They had to walk closer to the gym to get around all the inmates.

170

I met them halfway and said, "We're about to handle that *Phili* business in the chow hall right now. Should I call it off?"

Stomper's expression tightened for a split second. On each side of him, his henchmen turned to watch him.

Stomper said, "Call it off for today. We're rushing the Blacks right after the first lock up."

I nodded my head and said, "Boxer tried to get out here. He had me hold his door and yell for the tower to let me get back in but Garcia was watching."

Stomper nodded his head and smiled for a second. He predicted, "We'll both be in Solitary by the end of the day."

They turned and walked back to the bars.

I walked back to Damon and the rest of our group circled me. I said, "It's on and cracking after first lock up. Let them know not to get *Phili*."

We gathered in a line to work out on the curb while Gary squatted down and finger signed the message.

We worked out facing the yard doing burpies off the curb. I watched my brethren drop to do three pushups and pop back up before dropping and doing my set. We were a well-oiled unit watching everything while sweating out stress.

Across from us 40 yards, the Black inmates remained packed in their space watching everything. Some started playing dominoes. Some paced back and forth studying the yard for signs. A group of 20 plus Crip gang members started working out in a row like us.

They dropped to the ground for pushups and popped back up like an unstoppable military unit. All were big and shredded gangsters who were athletic and agile. They almost looked impossible to defeat.

Forty minutes into our routine, a few of the Black inmates broke from their group. I dropped down to do my 86th set of pushups and popped back up to see them start jogging.

Damon and the rest of our group dropped down for a set just as the Black inmates jogged past us.

The rest of the Black inmates were watching vigilantly to see how the Mexicans were going to respond.

The Black inmates jogged all the way around the track and made it back to their group. I found Tony in the mix shaking hands with the joggers. He broke from the group next and walked to the handball court.

Still, the rest of the Black inmates remained bunched up watching. The Crip gangsters who had worked out were watching closely. One of the oldest and biggest was in a squat position studying carefully as if he was determining the direction of the wind and if there was any tension being blown around.

The Mexicans all looked nonchalant. As if they didn't have anything planned.

At the handball court, on their side, a heated game was being played. Other Mexicans were on the sidelines keeping score. Others were hooting and hollering as if they were interested onlookers.

Other Mexicans were working out in lines at the pull up bars. Other Mexicans were jogging the track.

All looked normal.

The Black Crip gangster who was squatting down got up. Even from 40 yards away, I could see his expression register a decision that a riot wasn't on the agenda.

He gathered all the other Crip gangsters and held a meeting. A couple of minutes later a few of the Crip gangsters walked among the rest of the Black inmates giving orders. Then, their group started to venture into the rest of the yard.

There were over 30 Black inmates walking the track toward us.

Gary said, "I'm glad the yard isn't going to stay this full for long. It's suffocating."

The Black inmates walked past us and filled up the rows of pull up bars with the Asians. Past them, the Mexicans and Whites were using the rest of the bars. The rows of inmates waiting in line for a set stretched for 20 feet, only a few feet from the gym.

The guard in the tower above, held a block gun at the ready studying the yard carefully. His head rotated 180 degrees slowly, back and forth, like it was on a swivel.

Other Black inmates started playing basketball on half of the court, close to their territory on the yard.

The other half of the court, the side the Mexicans and Whites used, was empty.

Other Black inmates filled up space with the Asians at the handball court.

Tony ran past us in our corner alternating between running backwards and firing punches and skipping sideways.

Everyone heard the guard in the tower tap the microphone for an announcement.
"ATTENTION ON THE YARD! IN LINE!

YOU HAVE 5 MINUTES TO GET INSIDE!"

This was the moment of truth. How many Black inmates were going to go back inside the buildings?

At first, only a handful of Black inmates, mostly the older ones, headed for the opening vestibules.

Then, more started walking.

Damon said, "That's why we have mandatory yard."

Gary said, "They're going to get caught slippin."

More Black inmates left parts of the yard and walked back to their buildings.

I said, "More then half of them are going back inside. This isn't going to be fair."

Even most of the Crip gangsters were heading back inside.

The guard in the tower announced, "**YOU HAVE ONE MINUTE FOR INLINE!**"

Even more Black inmates went inside. There were less than 50 left. None of the Mexicans did. They still had over 300 at the ready for the surprise attack.

The sounds from the vestibules screeching and closing on each building with a resounding thud were replaced with a deathly tension.

The Mexicans got even quieter. They started bunching up in small groups.

Damon said, "Lets walk to our table."

We started walking the asphalt track slowly. Tony passed us jogging backwards and firing punches. A noxious feeling welled up in my stomach and started choking me. I wanted to warn Tony, but couldn't.

I looked back at the Black inmates left in their space by the tables. The big gangster Crip was back to studying everything intently, like he felt something coming.

Some of the Black inmates were at the tables playing dominoes. A dozen were at the handball court. Five more were using the pull up bars.

We got to the end of the track. Our White table was filled up with over a dozen Mexicans. The next table they used was also filled with watching Mexicans. All along the curb as the asphalt track turned and extended to the handball court, Mexicans were standing silently, waiting for a choreographed sign to move as one.

Then, it happened, some unseen sign took place and the Mexicans at our table and the next got up. They started walking into the yard.

The same thing happened with all the Mexicans standing along the curb down the track.

The Mexicans playing handball stopped. They also merged into the growing crowd walking into the middle of the yard.

Just past the handball court, over 300 Mexicans united. A small group broke apart and walked to the pull up bars where the Black inmates were working out amongst the Asians.

The rest of the Mexicans circled a wide arc around the other side of the handball court where the Blacks were congregating.

I saw Stomper standing tall among the front row of Mexicans. Then, the sea on inmates charged as one group with Stomper leading the way. The ground shook like an earthquake.

The Mexicans looked like army ants rushing the Black inmates. They were yelling like Indians during a raiding party. The screams ended as they got to Black inmates as the sounds of bodies colliding and punches took over.

Hundreds of Mexicans circled and overwhelmed small numbers of Black inmates. One Black inmate after another went to the ground and the stomping began.

Spilling out of the handball court and onto the asphalt track, Black inmates trying to defend themselves back pedaled toward Building 2 and 3.

One after another the surging Mexicans took them down in a heap. As each Black inmate hit the ground, the sea of Mexicans tightened in circles to deliver all out kicks, stomps and punches to their downed enemies.

Escaping, Tony was running backwards fast enough to escape for the moment. A separate army of over 30 Mexicans were chasing him, and gaining. A few who were sprinting all out led the way and fended through Tony's almost useless back pedaling punches.

Right as Tony ran out of space and his back slammed into the cement wall of Building 3, his Mexican adversaries landed the first hard punches. Tony's head slammed into the wall, his body lifted in the air as if climbing up it to escape and then the onslaught happened.

Both of Tony's hands fired impossibly fast punches to keep space for a few milliseconds. Then, his face absorbed punches from all sides and his head slammed back into the wall. The army of Mexicans squeezed in tighter, landing more punches and Tony went to the ground.

With an animal instinct, Tony popped up to fight back again. He fired more impossibly fast punches, only to get overwhelmed a second time by to many.

He went down again. This time he couldn't get up. Mexicans were kicking all out soccer style blows against his head. Others were stomping his face and body. Some were leaning down and firing punches.

His body jerked every time like a rag doll.

Tony tried to get up and took more blows and made it halfway up. Then, ruthlessly he was smashed back to the ground.

The alarm was screaming it's high-pitched whine up and down uselessly. In the background, as if it was in another life, the guard in the tower continued to scream, "***GET DOWN!! GET DOWN!! EVERYONE DOWN!!***"

Guards ran out of each building with block guns and canisters of pepper spray the size of small fire extinguishers.

A block gun exploded in front of us and never sounded so weak. The bullet hit the back of a Mexican bunched up around Tony.

The beating continued with screams and the sounds of blows landing.

The guards in the tower screamed with even more frantic energy, "*GET DOWN! GET DOWN! LIVE ROUNDS COMING NEXT!*"

Elsewhere on the yard, piles of Mexicans fit as tight as possible around fallen Black inmates.

Over by the pull up bars a number of Black men were still standing and firing punches. The 20 something Mexicans were having a hard time surrounding them.

The guard in the tower fired a live round at the ground near them and all the inmates went down.

To our left, the gate to D Yard opened and another army of over 30 prison guards from other yards rushed onto the scene holding block guns and pepper spray. More were running behind them.

The guards ran to where Tony was being beaten to death and fired one block gun after another. Other guards hosed orange pepper spray everywhere. One by one Mexicans separated from Tony and got on the ground.

Tony's survival instincts woke him up from unconsciousness and he crawled up and wobbled to his feet. He tentatively ran toward what he thought was safety but wasn't.

He entered the side of the handball court where most of the Mexicans were and got pummeled again.

Another army of Mexicans seized the opportunity and attacked him.

More block guns sounded, another live round sent dirt flying, and the war continued.

The Black inmates by the pull up bars realized other Black inmates were being murdered on the ground and began to run to help.

The yard was out of control. Tower guards from each building were dropping canisters of tear gas. Block guns were exploding uselessly and the one sided war continued.

Over 50 prison guards tried to get control of the Mexicans but were scared to get any closer. They stood close to the packs of inmates and sprayed pepper spray rather then completely engage.

Finally, the Mexicans started to get down in bunches. Others followed and got down. The guards closed in fast.

Then, like a rolling wave, a bunch of Mexicans got back up at the handball court. Screams of war were yelled and the insanity started again.

Black inmates who got up tried to fight back and were brought down again.

Lying next to me, Rocky said, "That's the LA Mexicans."

I noticed some of the fighting warriors and saw Capone kicking a Black inmate's head.

Next, another wave of Mexicans rose from the ground and went back to war.

Rocky said, "That's the Mexicans from San Diego."

They were getting up in different groups as counties to slam the victory home with emphasis.

Again the yard was out of control. Black inmates were fighting for their lives and staggering back to the ground.

More live rounds were fired, more impotent block guns sounded; more pepper spray was being hosed on inmates and painting them orange.

The guard in the main tower screamed, ***"GET THE FUCK DOWN! GET DOWN!"***

Tear gas rose from the ground in the 110-degree heat and it was finally over. We watched the guards close in and step on one inmate after another to add zip tie constraints.

We heard Black inmates, barely alive moaning in pain.

Lying next to me on the other side, Damon asked, "Where's the medics?"

I said, "Not until they have control of the yard."

Ten minutes later all the inmates were zip tie confined. We heard, **"CODE 4! SEND THE MEDICS."**

The End

Dear reader,

It is with sincere gratitude that I would like to thank you for reading **Down on the Yard**. I truly hope this book has been an eye opening experience. If you have enjoyed this book, please consider being kind enough to leave a review on Amazon. It would be helpful to other readers and me. Tap this link and scroll down about halfway on the left to where it says, want to leave a review~ http://www.amazon.com/dp/B00GVMSDS2 If you can share it on Facebook, Twitter or anywhere else I thank you! If you want one of my other books and can't afford it, I will gift one. You can contact me at rollcallthebook@gmail.com or friend me on Facebook to keep up with updates and praise reports here~ https://www.facebook.com/glennlangohrcalifornia

Would you rather listen to my books? Here is a complete list of my audio books~
http://amzn.to/1aeliPs

You can contact Glenn:
Author Page: http://www.amazon.com/-/e/B00571NY5A
Author Page UK: http://www.amazon.co.uk/-/e/B00571NY5A
Blog: http://rollcallthebook.blogspot.com/
Smashwords: http://www.smashwords.com/profile/view/lockdownpublishing.com
Facebook Pages:
https://www.facebook.com/glennlangohrcalifornia
https://www.facebook.com/lockdownpublishingdotcom
https://www.facebook.com/KindlePrisonStories
Twitter: https://twitter.com/#!/rollcallthebook